How to Land
in the Metaverse

How to Land   Crosby Studios
in the Metaverse
From Interior Design to the Future of Design

Harry Nuriev

New York · Paris · London · Milan

Harry Nuriev's work represents the definition of design in 2022. His work doesn't fit into any box—it's neither furniture nor architecture, it's not just Web3 or retail design. It's all of this, and most importantly, it's a vision.

Despite having started just a few years ago, there's something so unique in his work that perfectly captures our current world, living somewhere in between reality and the virtual. He found his specific codes very early on: the white and silver checkered pattern, the flashy monochromatic colorways—in shades of electric blue, acid green, or neon pink—along with materials like fake fur or transparent vinyl. With these elements as a palette, he then played around with them at will, like a child with their first letters of the alphabet, creating his unique vocabulary. Harry will always combine a certain naivety, a fresh impression, and his sharp eye to create his own culture.

Throughout the few projects we have worked on together, I've been amazed by Harry's professionalism and collaborative nature. For our *Just a Space* pop-up (see page 272), a temporary concept store launched in January 2022, Harry created an amazing rendering just for paper furniture, but he did not stop there: he came up with matching delicate paper flowers to accompany the space. These small, unexpected touches are the kind of magic that always make a difference. I'm looking forward to seeing what the next great inspirations for Crosby Studios' future projects will be, and I wish him the very best.

SARAH ANDELMAN

I believe that in order to make something truly amazing, you have to love it from the bottom of your heart. It doesn't matter if it doesn't match trends. If it feels good for you, then it's going to work. But it has to be 10,000 percent you. Why is this so important? I really don't know—this was my initial reaction when I decided to pursue what I'm doing now. At the time, another thought crossed my mind: people are so different, so individual, so why did so many interiors look the same? Quite often, rooms are either in the residential or hospitality sphere, and only belong to very specific style camps. With a desire to disrupt this notion, I launched Crosby Studios in 2014. I came up with my own visual language—transformism—which is based on rethinking and reevaluating the spaces and objects around us. Rather than creating more new things, I decided to take a look at what already existed, and to gauge what related to the existing style or simply to outdated furnishings. There's another element in my story: second chances. Why couldn't I just create something completely new? Why do I like to work sustainably? Well, why wouldn't I? It's time! Hi, I'm Harry Nuriev, and this is my book about the design language that I've been developing for the last decade.

HARRY NURIEV

Postcard from the Metaverse

by Samir Bantal

The Universe, all of us, have entered into live simulation.
—Baudrillard 1994[1]

VIEW OF THE MONT BLANC MASSIF, FRANCE, 2022

I've never been to the metaverse, yet it seems my life and your life are already being shaped in that realm. Unconsciously, a digital alter ego in its morula phase, growing as digital DNA strings trained on years and years of search engine—use behavior, screen time, and preferences, congregate to form virtual blocks of digital life. My virtual me knows me better than my real me. It predicts me better than my real me, but will it ever take over? For the first time, mankind is able to design and construct an immersive, parallel world, rather than inherit the one we live in. Designed for the disgruntled and disenfranchised, discontent with lethargic physical space, the metaverse is expected to outlive the internet an unlimited variety of spaces constructed by a binary code: "on" or "off." The fisheye lens is our gateway to this binary code space—straight lines become subtle curves. 3D goggles for virtual or mixed reality lock in our retinas for uninterrupted attention, shrinking the space between headset and eyeball. Designer-artist Harry Nuriev did not get involved in the virtual world by coincidence, as the latest idea of this internet society, but as part of modern man's long-lasting wish for a parallel, virtual, fantasy world—one you can visit but also leave. Nuriev's work, both real and virtual, signals a new generation of designers that anticipates a virtual future and claims it as their new world to explore—a future where we could spend more time in our virtual fantasies than in reality.

Long before Meta's metaverse, virtual reality had been envisioned by Stanley G. Weinbaum in *Pygmalion's Spectacles* nearly a century prior.[2] The short story starts with the opening line "But what is reality?" Weinbaum's version of the virtual was photographed in a liquid with light-sensitive chromates, taste was chemical, sound electrical. Touch? Simply supplied by the mind. Weinbaum's description of virtual reality goggles is very accurate to today's definition of VR goggles. The main character questions the illusion as it made reality, as he knew it, almost unbearable. Soon he desperately wanted this version of reality not to stop. Published in 1935, Weinbaum's version was a concept built on a stereoscope from the early 1800s. Two mirrors at

HARRY NURIEV AND SAMIR BANTAL, 2022

WINDOW CHAIR, 3D RENDERING, 2022

forty-five degrees to the user's eyes reflected an image located off to the side. Fused inside the brain, a three-dimensional image is then accepted by the brain. The Great Exhibition in 1851 spiraled the stereoscope into the first global virtual 3D industry. Unreachable places were captured on these View-Master predecessors. Fantasy worlds soon followed. Slivers of TV displays replaced silver plates. Realistic images and sound effects, developed by the gaming industry, are gaining on Weinbaum's *Pygmalion's Spectacles.*

The term *metaverse* was first coined in 1982 by Neal Stephenson in his novel *Snow Crash.*[3] Here, the metaverse, depicted as an urban environment, a single hundred-meter-wide street, ran the circumference of a perfectly black and featureless spherical planet. The main character, a hacker, travels between twenty-first century postapocalyptic Los Angeles and the metaverse. Often cited by many entrepreneurs and inventors as Silicon Valley's "inspiration," it is not surprising that we have adopted the name of a dystopian version of a fantasy world as the new digital promise after the internet. In *Snow Crash* the metaverse concept is an uninspiring, predictable, shallow virtual world to escape dystopian reality of a world dominated by big tech corporations. The irony is unreal.

Today's metaverse is still more fantasy than reality, except that it is being constructed for pleasure and entertainment to escape reality and offer an alternative to reality. A simulacrum, where reality is replaced by a simulation. In here, reality ceases to exist. Or does it? Typically, words construct dreamscapes faster than the hand can make them. We surrender to scripted hallucinations, conscious forms of dreaming—timeless, spaceless . . . limitless. Will we be truly happy in a limitless world? Digital trickery as an imposed perpetual reality. Sensations are mental phenomena, reality can't be proven, so who cares if the optical illusion is real? It is the mind that Harry designs for. He exploits our mind's ability to form the space before it's constructed or obsoletes even the construction itself.

GREEN BATHROOM, 3D RENDERING, 2020

CUBIC CHAIR, 3D RENDERING, 2020

FLORAL-PRINT OFFICE CHAIR, 2020

When Facebook changed its name to Meta, it sent out a clear message: the metaverse is the future. Not only social media but also the complete online universe would slowly transition to the metaverse. A domain that still has not been "designed" or even defined in detail, but lives as a collection of ideas and concepts, all taking place in virtual spaces. By being first, Meta tries to define the metaverse. Ironically, right now the concept of a metaverse could live in each and every one of us, but a single company, or a small number of tech companies, will eventually dictate its fundamental principles of "neo-physics," when we replace space, time, and gravity with attention as its currency. By embracing the concept of the metaverse or any virtual universe, Nuriev could lift the ambivalent veil that tech companies are not able to crack. Will he and his peers, artists and designers using gaming software and ultra-realistic rendering programs, serve us the alternative reality to a reality that has never been able to offer us inclusivity or safety, while staying playful, unpredictable, and risky?

As a third of the world's population plays video games as a form of pastime, more than half of the world's businesses work remotely, and a projected six billion people will use social media in 2027, more and more memories are created in a virtual world. But where the online world is now mainly used for pure communication, the metaverse will add a third dimension—worlds "we" experience in high definition as a form of temporary retreat from reality. Metaverse plans to be the permanent retreat from reality, a new reality. An alter reality. Even though we haven't figured out how to avoid a voluntary form of digital escapism, monetized to become a permanent transactional incarceration, escapism itself, being physical or mental—whether or not it's augmented by hallucinogens—has been a fundamental part of shaping our alter states and perhaps mankind's secret formula to immortality. Retreat as a form of survival. The metaverse serves our alter egos more than our real egos. An altered society. It's a society that is optional. Nuriev does not seem to be interested in the metaverse as an end state but much more in the exploration of the virtual as an equal to the real. The metaverse is his lab. It is critical that designers and artists claim this territory before it turns into Stephenson's dystopian reality: a linear and cynical fantasy.

Soft voiced, Harry tells me about his first explorations of the virtual. Born in 1984, halfway between the Black Sea and the Caspian Sea, in a country (the USSR) that today only exists in history, Harry was initially trained as an architect before he switched to interior design. Growing up as a child in the administrative town without internet or magazines, Harry used fantasy to reimagine spaces as smooth, monochromatic environments. "Virtual reality is an exercise machine" as Harry put it. It started from his interest in paper architecture—a virtual form of architecture, well before architecture evolved from existing on a white page to existing on a black screen—as a form of ultimate freedom. The virtual opened a universe of experimentation. It is a form of rejecting reality. A rejection of the mundane. Esthetically pleasing as form of mental healing or even a spatial aphrodisiac. Architecture is an extensive avoidance of limitations held together by a dream.

During the Soviet part of Harry's life, international travel was virtually impossible, forcing him to explore the *virtual* in the greatest metaverse known: fantasy. The virtual became the metaphysical environment that allowed him to travel as often and as far as possible, imagining esthetics loosely defined by color and the absence of material. Dematerialization becomes the trademark of the virtual. Polygons as moldable building blocks. Abstracted surfaces as an architectural universal language. Harry has not surrendered to the inevitability of the virtual, yet Harry travels between real and virtual. He gives us a glimpse of how these worlds could actually run parallel. Like a Rekall trip, we become Douglas Quaid,[4]

CROSBY BEDROOM, 3D RENDERING, 2020

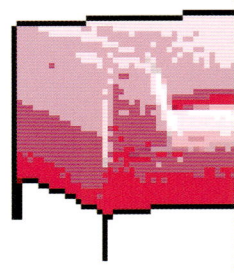

PIXEL SOFA, 2022

"Nuriev does not seem to be interested in the metaverse as an end state but much more in the exploration of the virtual as an equal to the real."

BLUE OUTDOOR BENCHES, 3D RENDERING ON PHOTO, 2021

PRINTER DRESSER, 2018

AT CROSBY HQ, 2021

"These spaces can either be real or not, here or there at the same time. Color becomes protagonist, creator, and executioner in a neutralized world."

who visits Rekall to have a memory of visiting a new world, Nuriev sends us off into a physical representation of a digital space, or is it the other way around? A perfect dream state, we don't need goggles nor screens to experience it, we step into Harry's digital rendering, and we can step out any time we want. In the slipstream of space, fashion is the next domain for our digital alter reality, that, like architecture, has not yet made a viable contribution to digital maturity as the internet. Within reach, fashion is Nuriev's next world to explore.

In his earlier works, gray-white checkerboard backgrounds—commonly used in rendering programs as a tabula rasa, an unmaterialized, fluid space without identity—cover spaces Harry wants to dematerialize, unleashing its potential by stripping it from any form of recognition. These spaces can either be real or not, here or there at the same time. Color becomes protagonist, creator, and executioner in a neutralized world. The checkered pattern is the only placeholder color or material accepted as definite. Material is loading . . . color is loading . . . never reaching 100 percent, destined to remain a limbo interior.

Well before reality, there is fantasy. Harry decides when and if that fantasy materializes. He started constructing with what he calls the smallest of architectural elements: furniture. My first encounter with Harry's work was his lounge chair. A sharp-edged metal cube, missing two adjacent surfaces, substituted with soft seating, an enticing simplicity. Not sure if what I had Googled was real or a rendering, I reached out to Harry. He replied he could have it produced. If it was a rendering, I was convinced it was real, if it was a real, I doubted its existence. But what did exist first was the virtual representation of this idea. A part of Harry's work is intentionally "unreal." Perfectly aware of media being predominantly digital, Harry knows his work will be consumed from a screen device to be sent to our eyes. We see a pixelated image, smoothed in our brain. Digital trompe l'oeil fools us into recognizing a familiar language, especially to architects-designers, that this space is merely digital . . . but also real. Resolution serves as our brains' lubricant to accept images we know are not fully developed. Low-res furniture, in "preview-mode" spaces, prove we don't need a device to enjoy virtual esthetics nor do we need finalized images to interpret intentions. We possess the most powerful "device" already: our brain.

Smoothness is Harry's motive for the rejection of the mundane as the semiotics of a generation that avoids conflict and blurs lines of opposition by reframing the binary codes of modern life to vectoral explorations. In urbanism, the marriage of the digital and the physical is based on the doctrine of smoothness or effortlessness. The digital is a soft, warm blanket that shields us from any discomfort, fed to us by algorithms that predict our desires faster than we can imagine them. Will there be any discomfort or challenge in the metaverse? Discomfort is the equivalent of an electromagnetic force that thrusts an object into movement by preventing it from reaching a stationary balance. Scientists at Wageningen University in the Netherlands that specialize in life sciences and agricultural sciences have proven that even plants that live in too much comfort become lazy and weak, decreasing their chance of survival.[5] Just like too much stress kills, too much comfort kills. Harry's smooth spaces, however, are not to be mistaken for comfort. The enticer-designer arouses hope that the virtual is real. It's the enticement that makes Harry's version of the metaverse a perfect escape. Infinite scrolling in 3D, wandering through spaces that invite us to stay a bit longer or never leave.

Harry defines his work as *transformism—trans*, a Latin prefix meaning "beyond or "across," and *form*, the physical world he explores and experiments with. In the science of evolution, transformism is the ability of one species to change to another. In order to become virtual, we need transformism. From the real to the virtual . . . and back. Harry's work serves as an embassy of the virtual, stripped from the mundane but open-ended by its dematerialization. It demonstrates that there is a limbo world to be explored by designers, artists, and thinkers before it is occupied by Big Tech's array of *attention surplus disorders*. Where the virtual reality is the full digital replacement of vision, augmented reality (AR) overlays a digital layer of data on top our vision of reality. AR has found its way into our phones and our lives in a more subtle way when in 2016 Niantic launched Pokémon GO. Virtual creatures, located, captured, trained, and battled through our mobile devices, successful not only for its dopamine-based reward system but because real and recognizable spaces were suddenly transformed into an exciting virtual universe. People chased virtual creatures to their own fatal ends. AR, though, can only exist with reality as its basis, denying the option to erase reality. Harry introduces a "bi-reality" that is real and digital, simultaneously. You can visit and explore both or reject both. He introduces an alternative reality to the inevitability of the digital as a transitional moment and refines his vocabularies of *nowhere*—an innocent reality where consent replaces force. A digital reality that lives as a simulation in physical space, while the digital space is occupied with "photo-realistic" environments that sometimes seem too good to be true, that you want to be true.

Harry sends me a WhatsApp photo from his trip to Chamonix. It's our modern version of a postcard, an instant postcard from the digital age. In the photo, a window frames the French mountain landscape from above. High above the mountaintops, Harry's room seems to be flying high in the sky. Is this real?

1. *Simulacra and Simulation*, Jean Baudrillard, 1981, Semiotext(e).
2. *Pygmalion's Spectacles*, Stanley G. Weinbaum, 1935, Createspace Independent Publishing Platform.
3. *Snow Crash*, Neal Stephenson, 1992, Bantam Books.
4. *Total Recall*, film by Paul Verhoeven, 1990.
5. *Countryside: A Report*, Rem Koolhaas & AMO, 2020, Taschen.

HOUSE IN CALIFORNIA, 2020

DESIGN FOR VIDEO GAME, 2022

Samir Bantal is an architect, curator, and the director of AMO, a research and design studio at OMA, a renowned Dutch architecture office founded by Rem Koolhaas. AMO works in fields crucial to architecture, such as media, technology, and culture.

VIRTUAL

PROJECTS

01 META HOUSE
24–39

02 META WORKSHOP
40–51

03 PARIS ATELIER
52–57

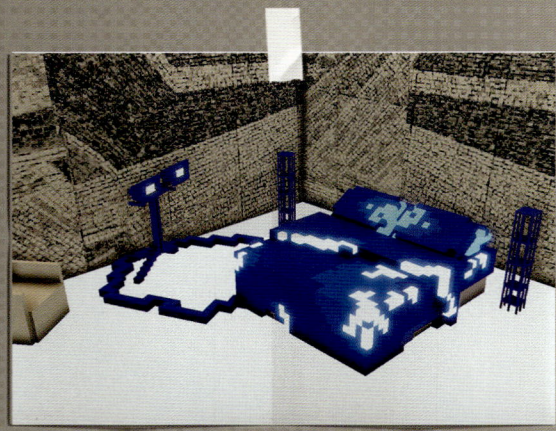

04 CROSBY VIDEO GAME
58–67

05 FLYING HOUSE
68–77

06 RV
78–85

07 COVER STORY
86–91

08 VIRTUAL KITCHEN
92–97

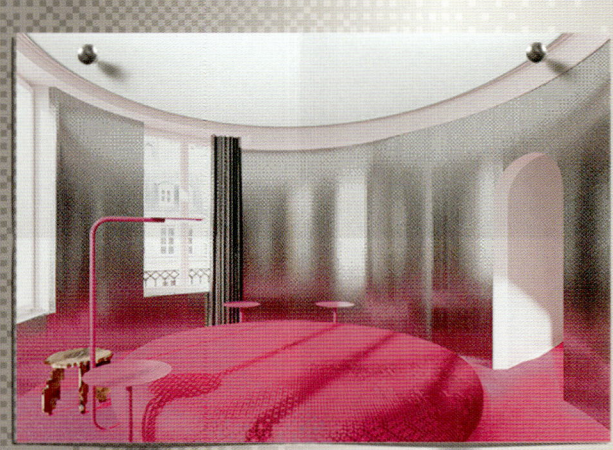

09 PARIS HOTEL
98–107

10 NIKE SOFA
108–113

Meta House, 2022

When I first started designing virtual spaces, I didn't have any idea what the meta world was. It simply didn't exist back then. But, a few years later, I figured out that my 3D renderings were actually a part of the real world. Well, not "real" but real in my daily work, which has absolutely no limit. How surprised I was when I realized that unlimited creative freedom is scary, and that it was actually blocking my hands in moving forward. Interior designers and architects are born and raised to always solve issues and to turn obstacles into opportunity. It's just our nature—to make the impossible possible. When you don't have any limits, you actually don't have motivation. You are simply bored. So, barriers are good if you have a key to open them. It's never just about visuals—everything is based on investing in something, solving issues, and transforming obstacles into opportunity. When you touch the virtual world, there aren't any issues, there's nothing to solve. Everything is critically clear, or to use another word, endless with emptiness. I found this to be problematic, and filled out these digital spaces with my fantasy.

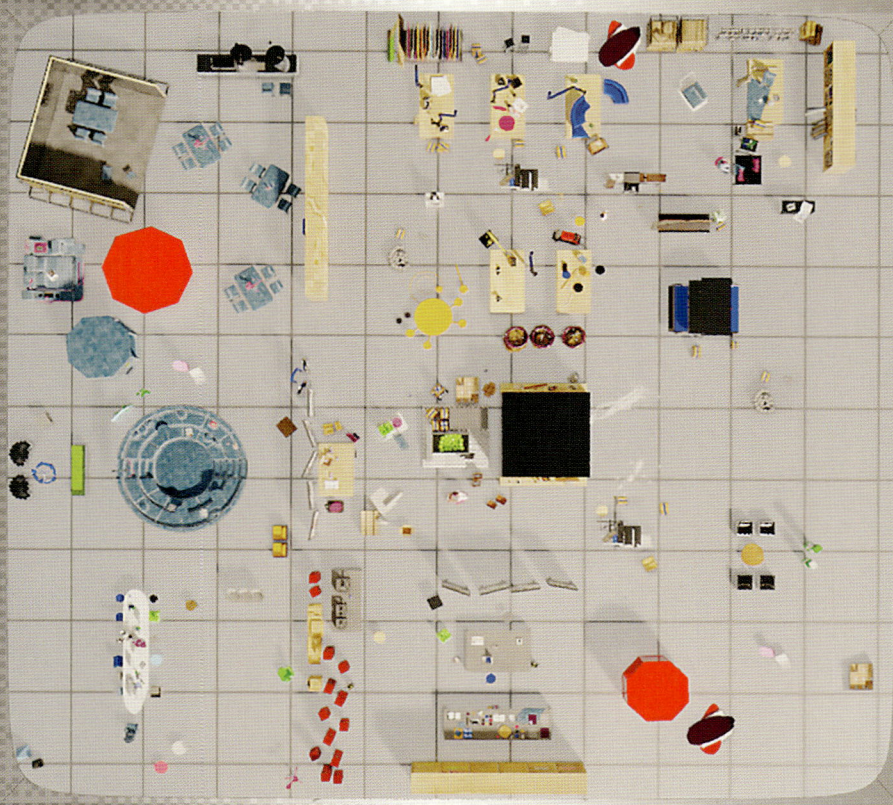

Meta Workshop, 2022

Producing my objects is not the same thing as creating and designing them. Once an idea comes to the factory, it's going to face some obstacles in terms of time and materials. But when you create or dream, there are no limits. What if there was a workshop where we could build every idea that comes to mind in a second, without a question? I was dreaming about this utopia of a perfect design world for individuals who work with furniture and objects. After visiting many carpenters and production factories, I found that they were always behind a screen. However, with this dream project, they can see the start-to-finish process from idea to object in a fun, entertaining environment.

Paris Atelier, 2022

I remember the time when, if you wanted to talk with someone, you could just give them a call and when you wanted to see someone you could just swing by and knock on their door to say hello. I remember this very well. Now, we have to make appointments and schedule calls, and it still doesn't mean you are going to meet in-person. I designed a virtual space, my atelier in Paris, that you can visit without filling out forms, sending e-mails, and waiting for any reason. What are these blue walls made of? It's denim! And why not denim? I like to dress my spaces, not decorate them.

Crosby *Video Game*, 2022

I never really played video games when I was kid, except for *The Sims*, which allows you to simulate your home. Technically, I didn't play it—I was just building my interiors by choosing the walls, furniture, and windows. It was very fascinating. The idea of this *Video Game* project came from these memories. I thought that it would be so nice to play with design by combining different objects using the signature Crosby Studios language. Also, in a world of unbelievably realistic video games, I wanted to play with 1990s graphics, where everything is purely pixelated and you barely can distinguish a planter from a stool. This game also inspired me to create a new furniture collection.

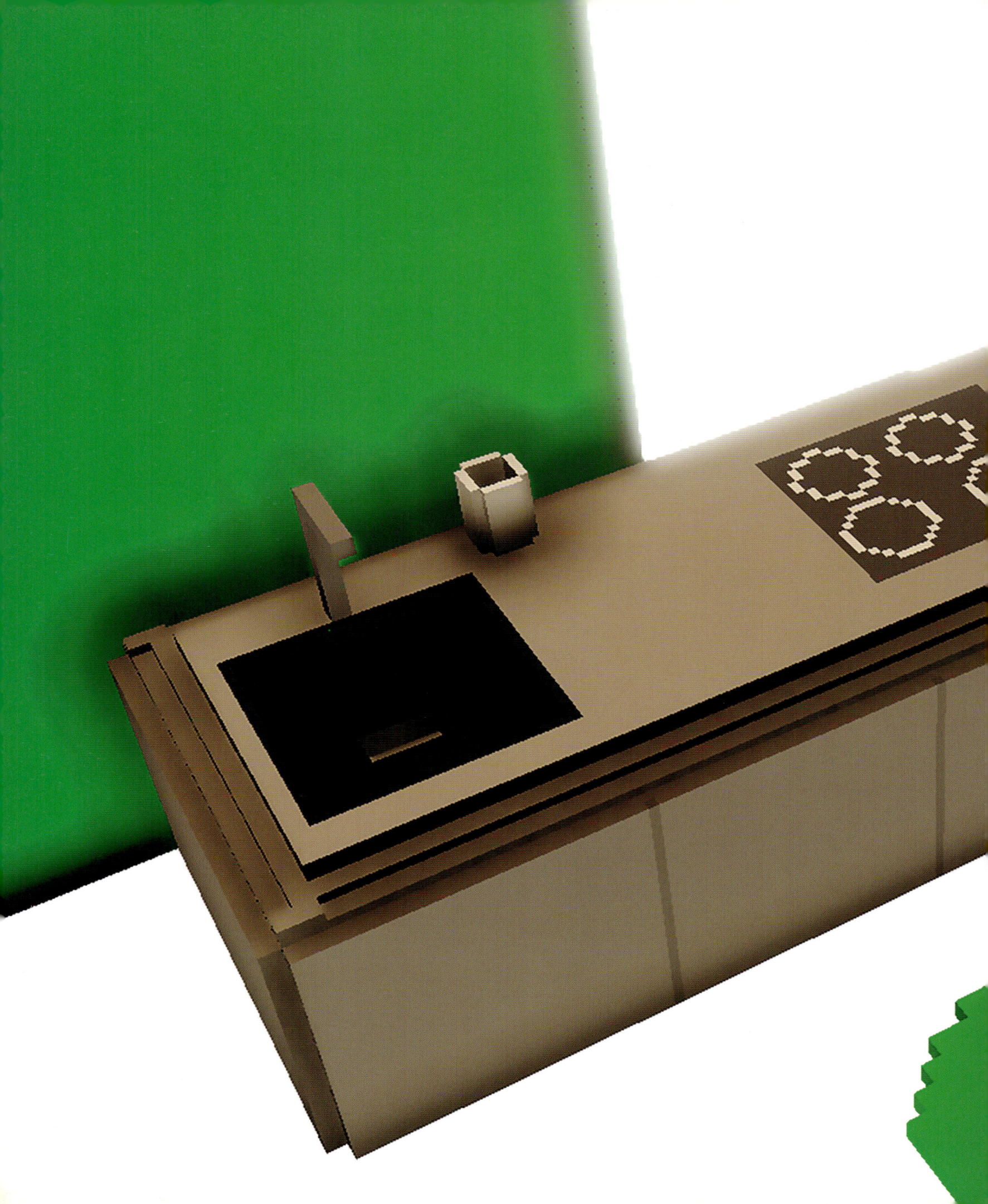

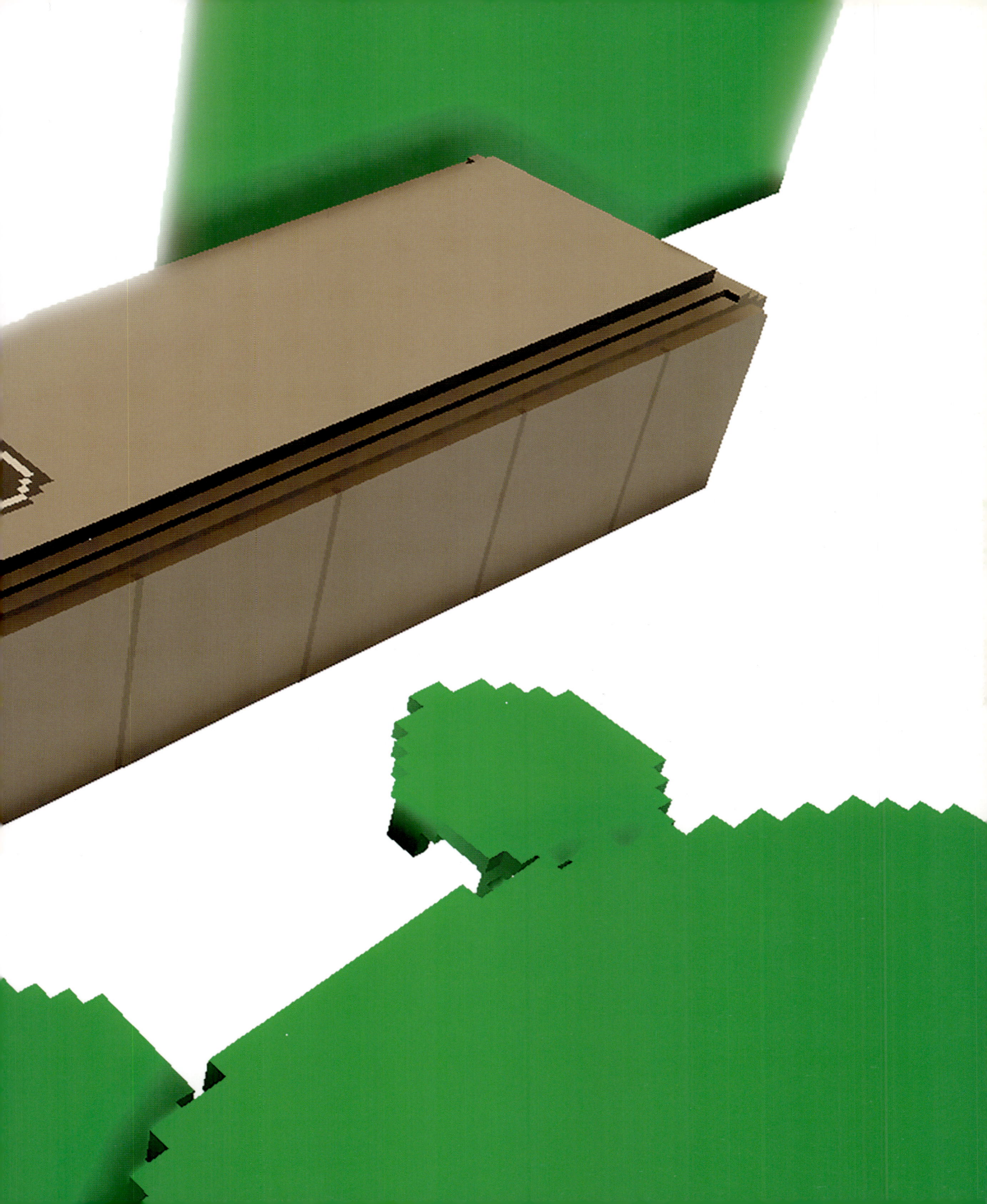

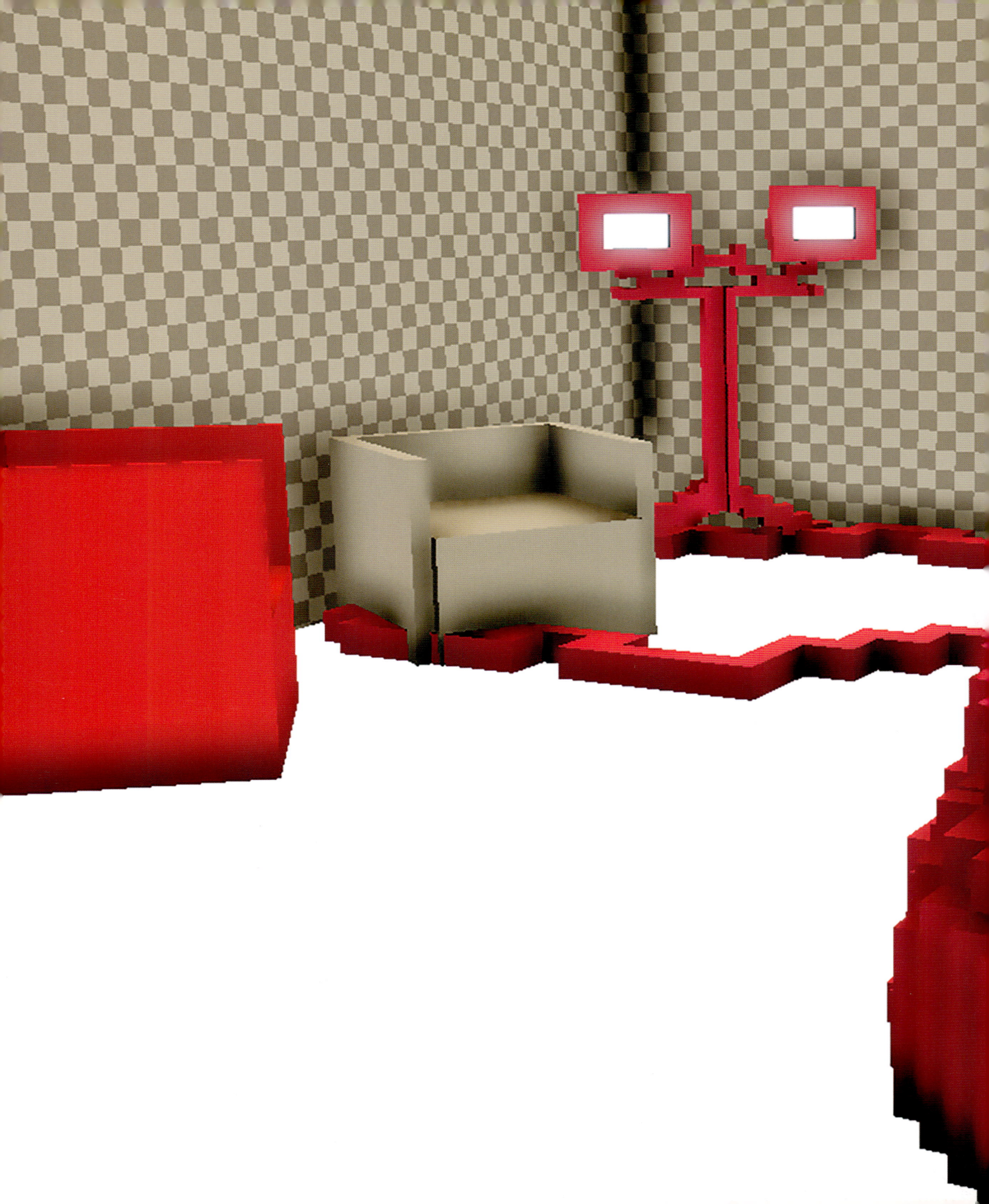

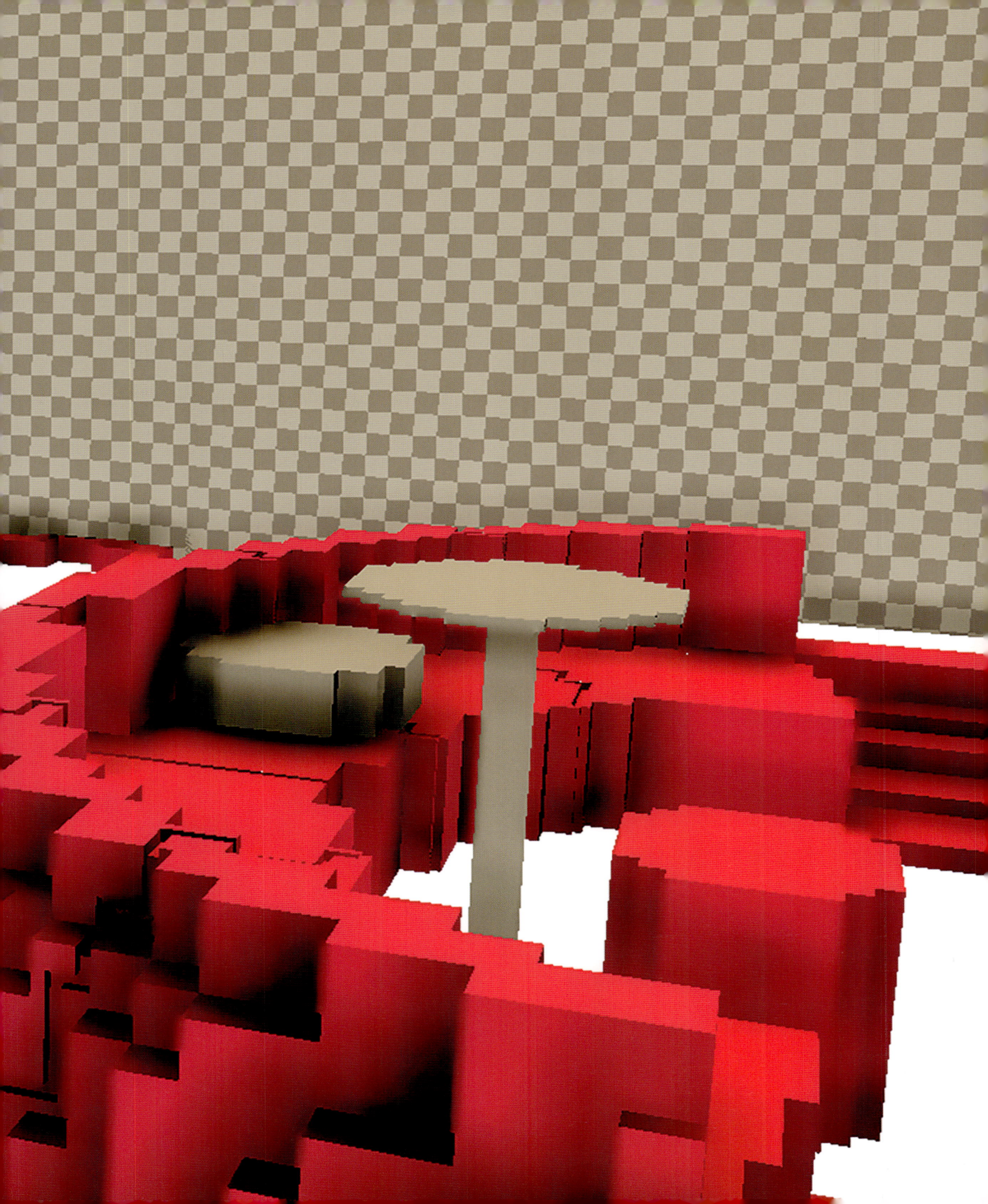

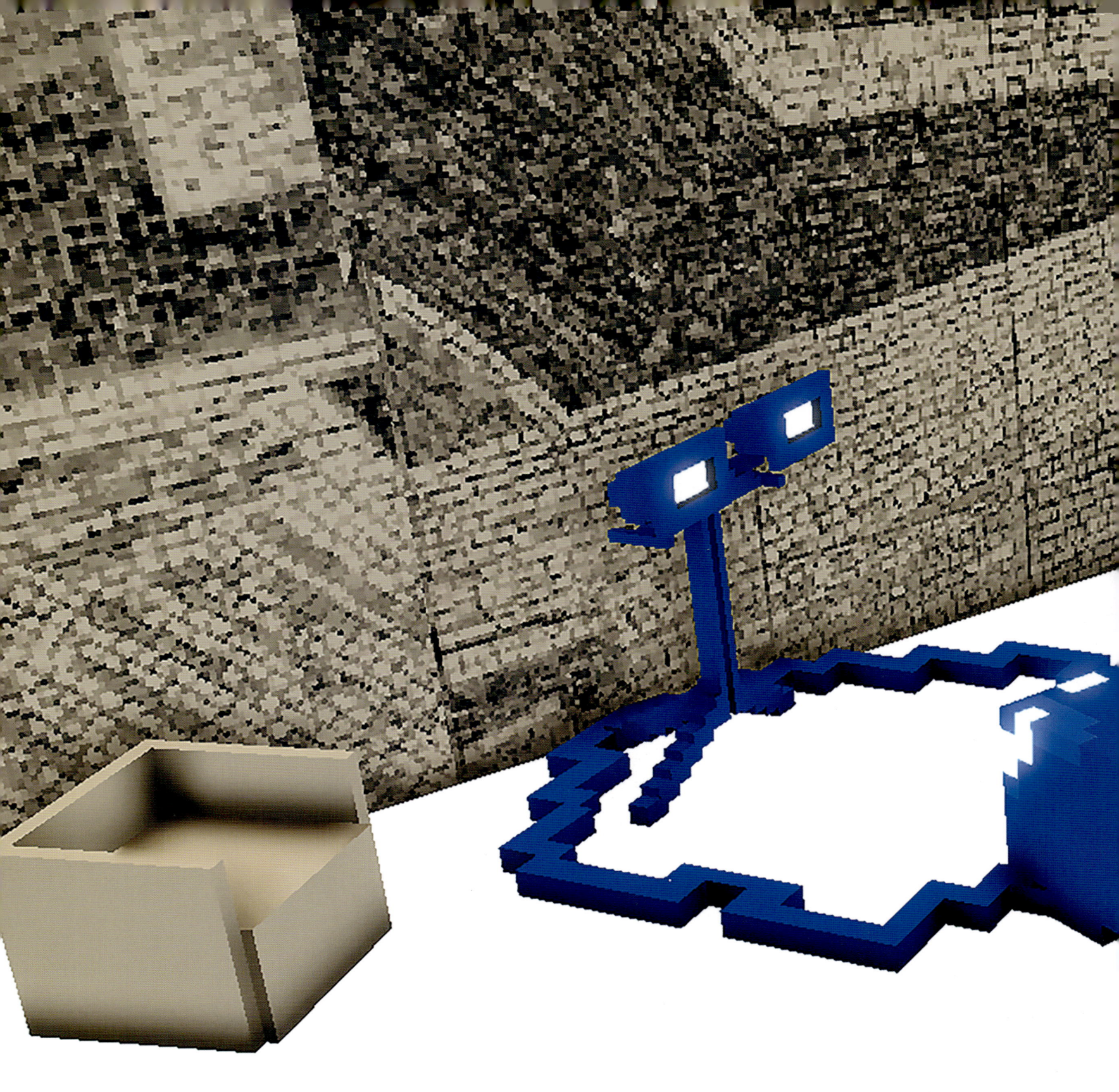

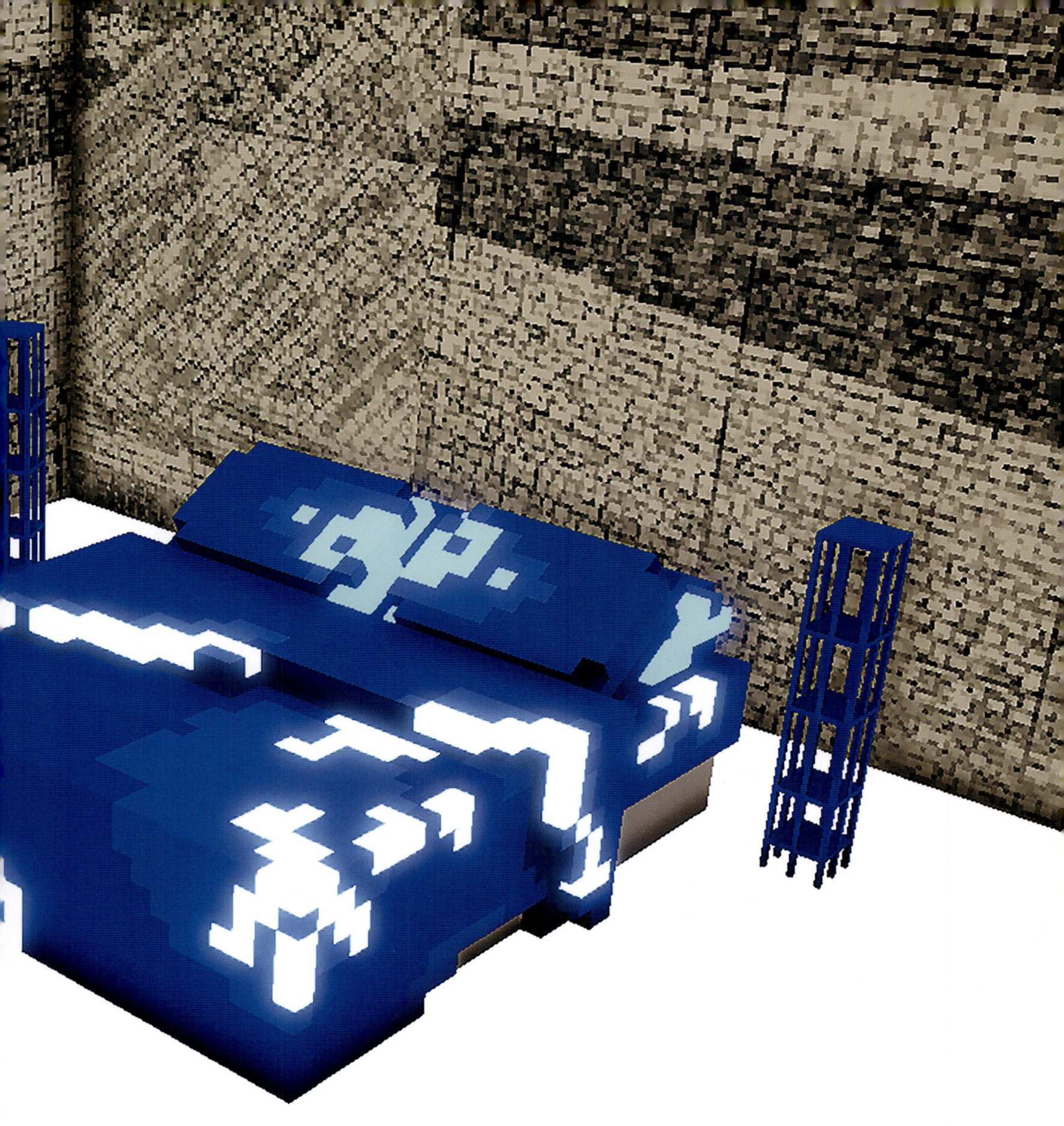

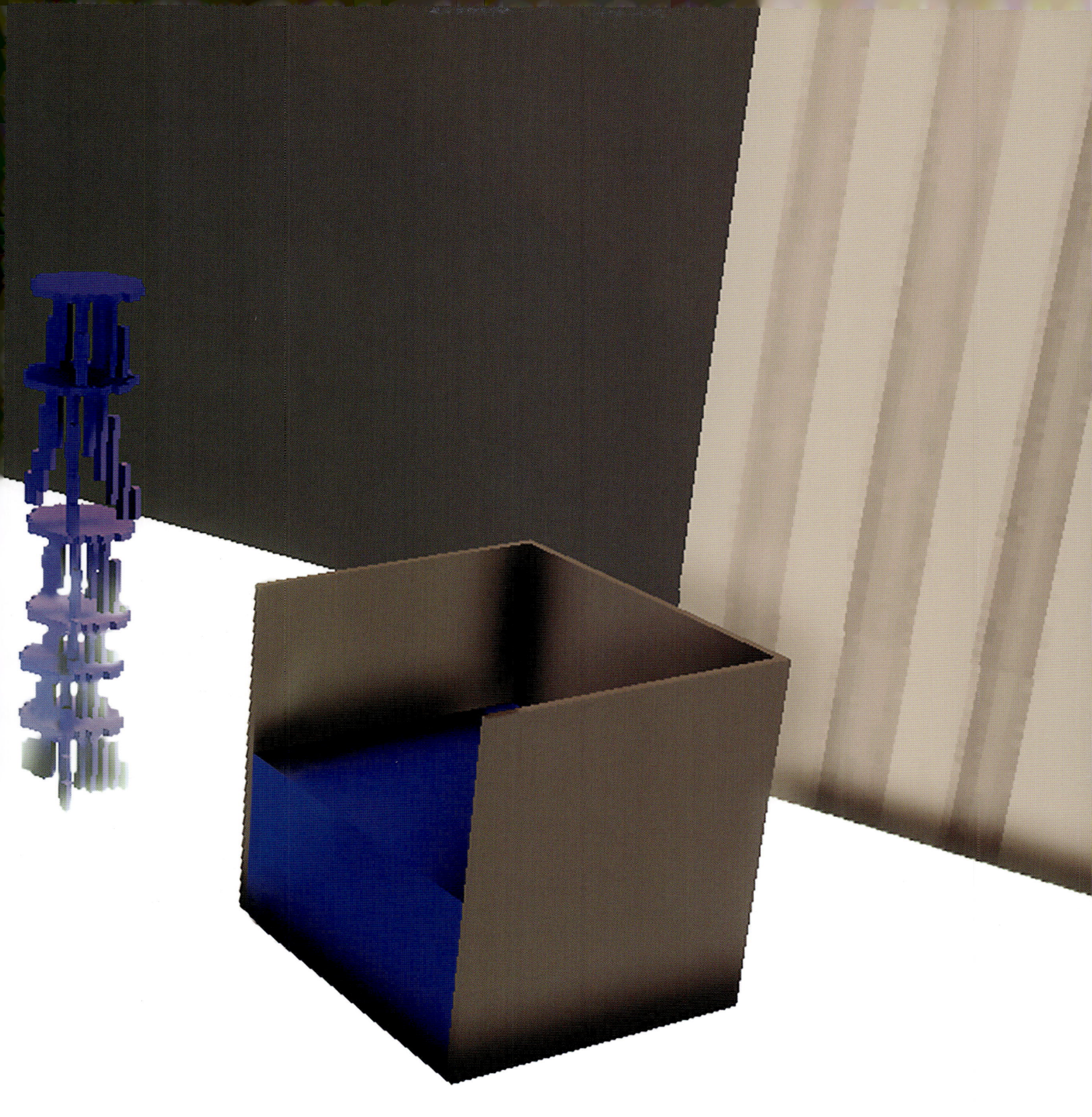

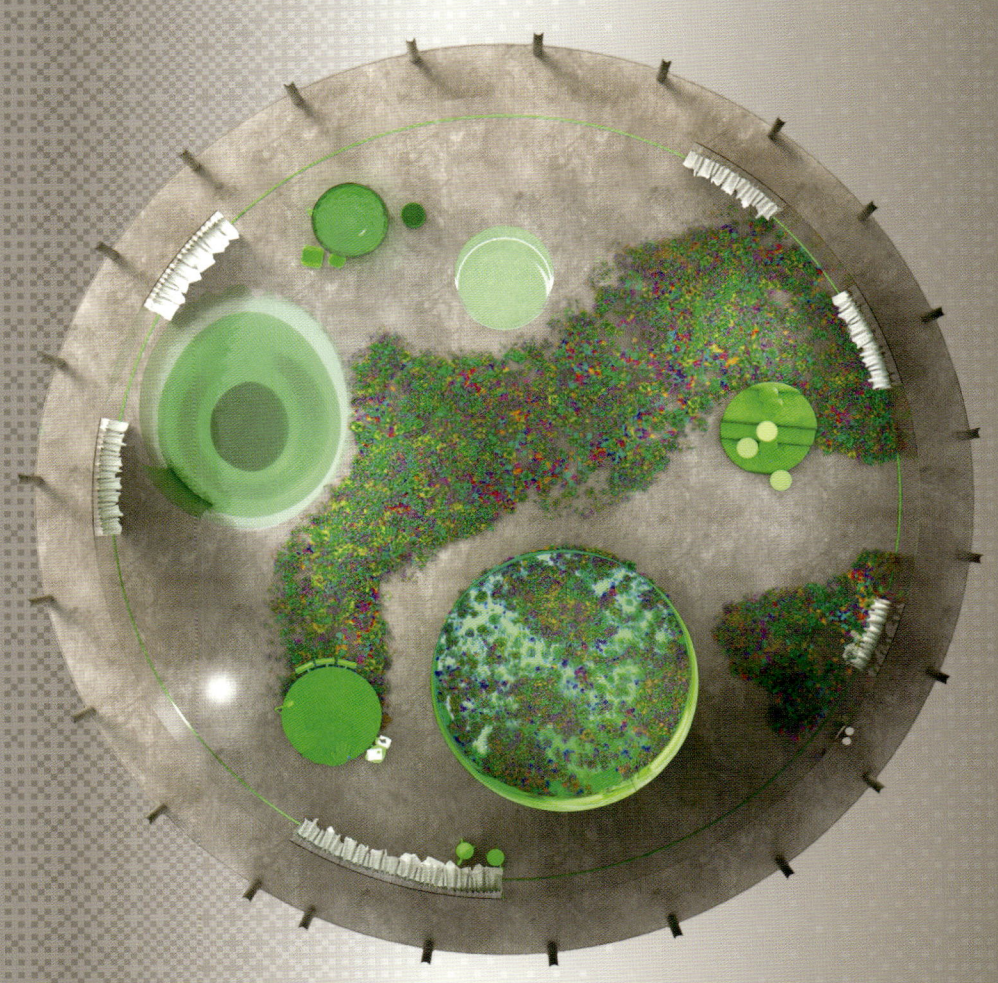

Flying House, 2021

The concept of *Flying House* was based on my travel and life experience. When you travel a lot and are changing time zones every month, at some point you disengage with daily reality and become a "no-land" person. It's very romantic, but also very uncomfortable. When you live out of two suitcases and travel from one bed to another and don't drink your tea from your favorite mug it becomes part of your identity. This house reflects the fantasy of having your home follow you everywhere you go. My installation evokes the idea of how to bring natural landscapes inside the house, showing that instead of just a bunch of planters you can capture an authentic outdoor feeling.

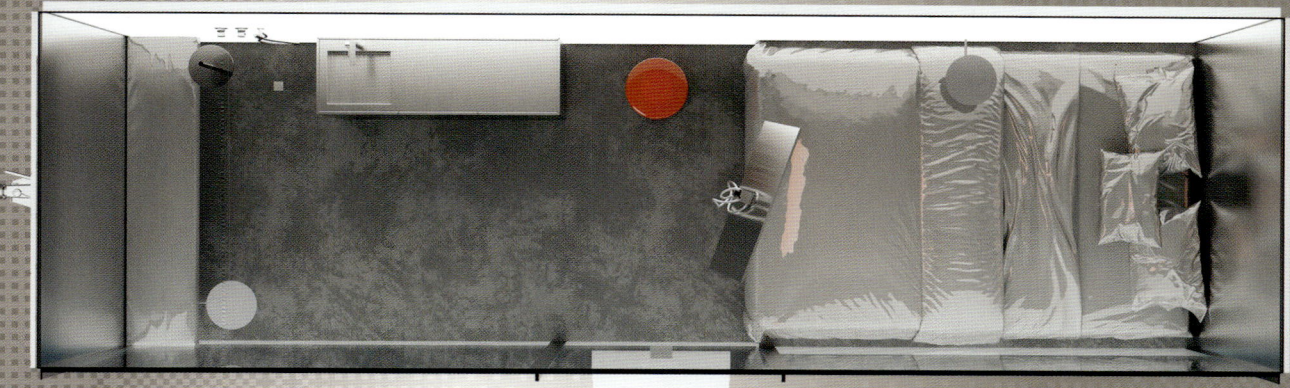

RV, 2021

This is a very important project for me. The concept of an RV was inspired by my lifestyle—or the lifestyle I'd love to have. I've been traveling so much these last five years, regularly taking over one hundred flights in a span of twelve months. I started losing my feeling of home. Well, I actually lost it completely. I didn't know where my clothes, books, or favorite nail clippers were. This prompted the idea to create a portable home, or RV, that I could travel around the world in, with the most important things in my life—which, it turns out, I don't need that often.

Cover Story, 2020

Here, I worked on a transition from the world of sneaker heads to the world of interior design. My challenge was to take the colors and surfaces from sports shoes and to transform them into living spaces. It was one of my first virtual projects. I was reminded that no limit can sometimes be a limit as well. Virtual projects train you to think without any physical aspects, and it can be quite challenging.

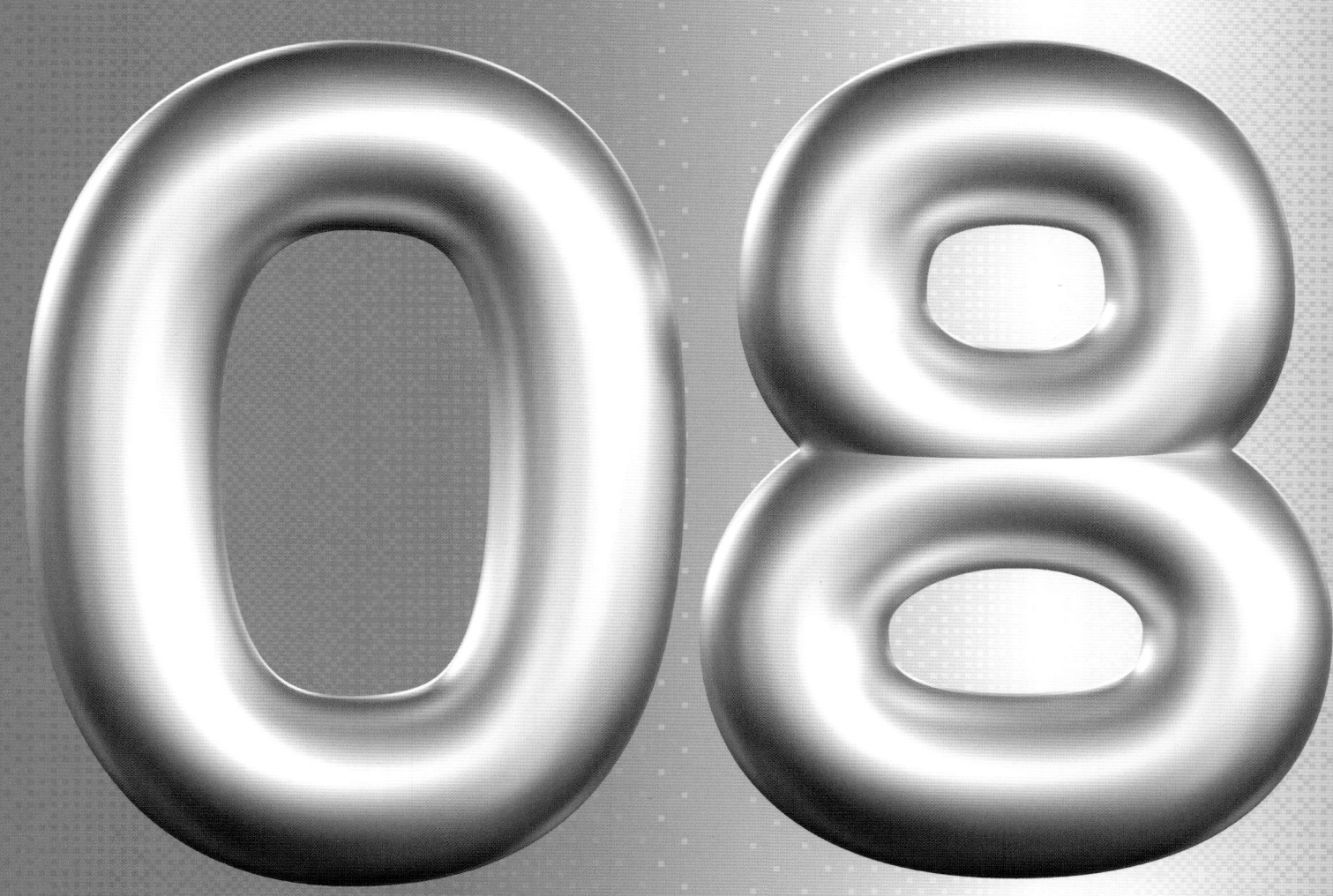

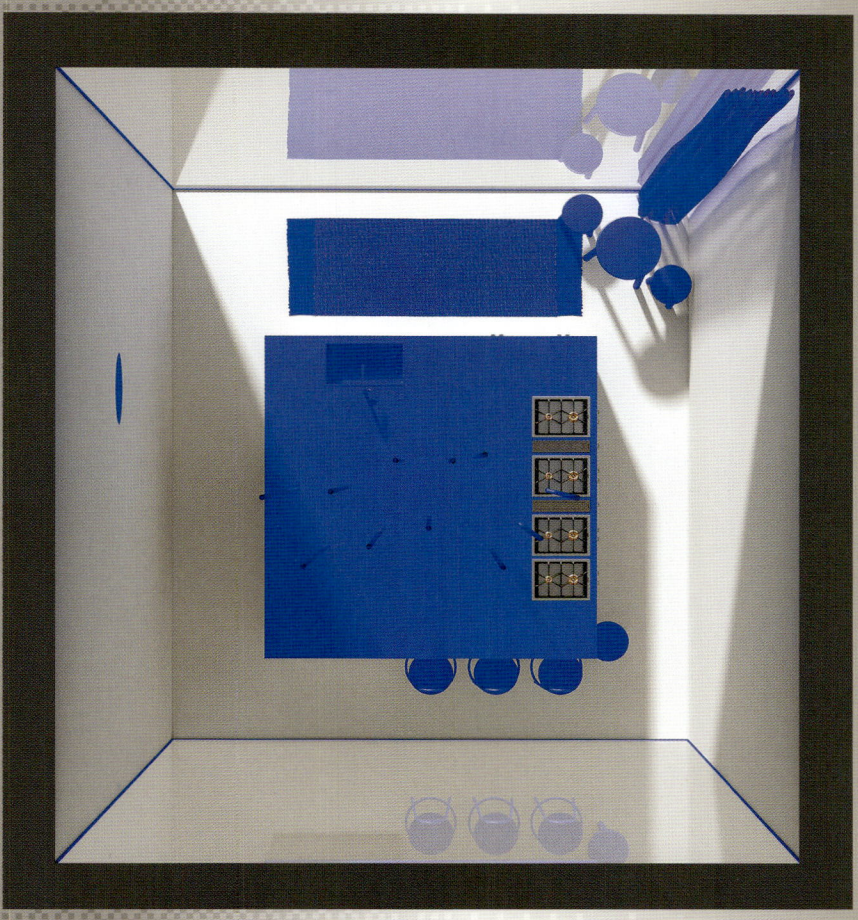

Virtual Kitchen, 2020

In general, kitchens are sacred rooms. Think back to making decisions, or having intimate conversations and thoughts, in your or someone else's kitchen. Things that you say or think in the kitchen can be different than when you are in other room. The act of cooking food for yourself or someone you love is as important as eating. I love kitchens for these reasons, and honestly they are the most important room for me in any house. Kitchens also exude the energy of a laboratory . . . pure creation.

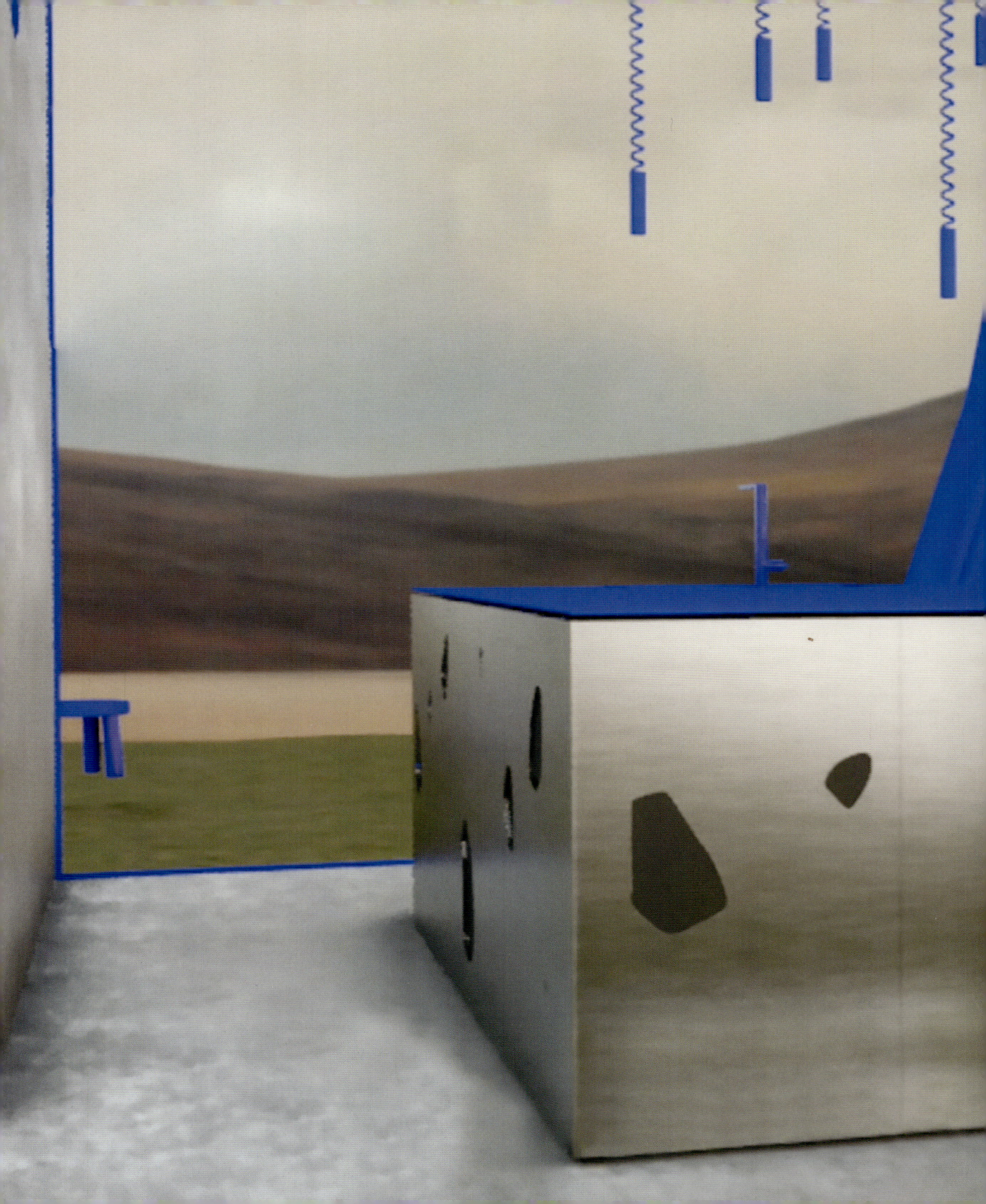

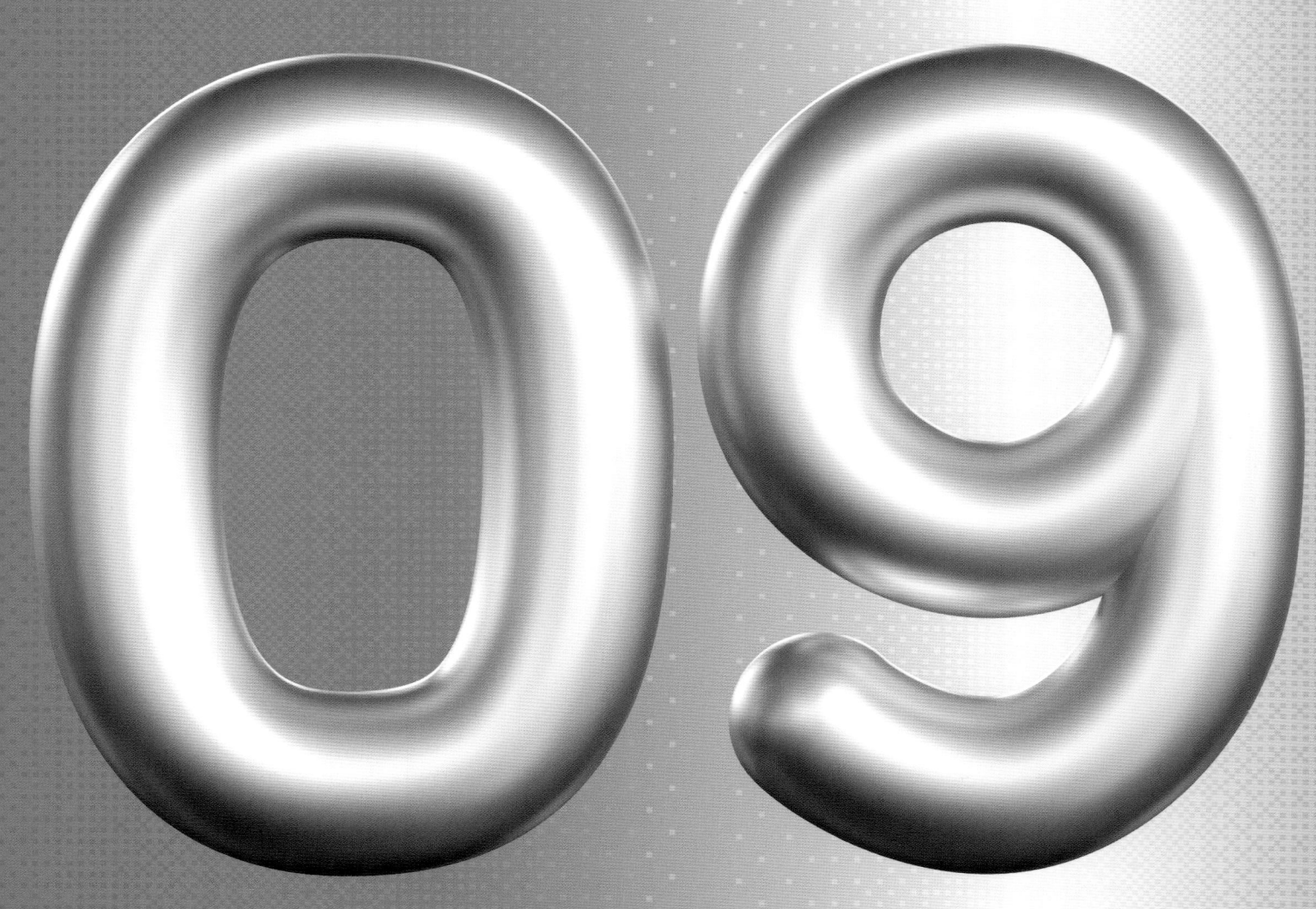

Paris Hotel, 2022

As a genre, I think hotels are on a different level. Hospitality is now something in-between your private home and a rental property. I think back to Le Corbusier's dreams of the future; he said that people would have wall tapestries instead of oil canvas paintings so that the artworks could be easily rolled down and moved to a new place—a sort of anchor-less life. This hotel project is unique because I designed one room at a Paris hotel in real life and another one in virtual reality at the same time. You can visit the room physically and through your headset. You might ask me, Why would I visit the virtual hotel? Isn't the point of travel to sleep in a real hotel? Well, I spend so many nights in hotels and I can affirm that once in a while you just want to be home. And then, back at home, sometimes you have the fantasy of traveling.

Nike Sofa, 2020

The first time I collaborated with Nike, they wanted me to think about their Air Max sneaker in an unusual way. It was a fun challenge. Instead of thinking toward sports and athletes, I came up with a furniture collection. One of my objects was an armchair. How does it relate to the fashion brand? I believe the designer of Air Max once said that in order to create sneakers you should create a chair first. So, I decided to create a chair out of sneakers. I understand why he wanted to experiment with furniture—it has a different function and it really informs your thoughts. With this project, I decided to make a sofa out of puffer jackets that exist only in the virtual world.

REAL WORLD

PROJECTS

11 PARISIAN HOME
118–131

12 PURPLE DUPLEX
132–141

13 BROOKLYN APARTMENT
142–151

14 BABY BLUE SPACE
152–157

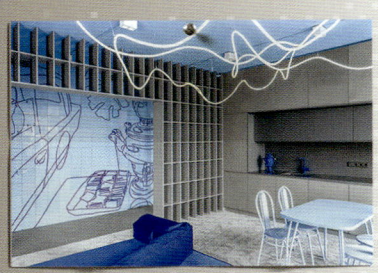

15 BLUE STUDIO
158–163

16 ROOM WITH BED CAPSULE
164–169

17 SILA SVETA SPACE
170–177

18 ZERO10 POP-UP
178–185

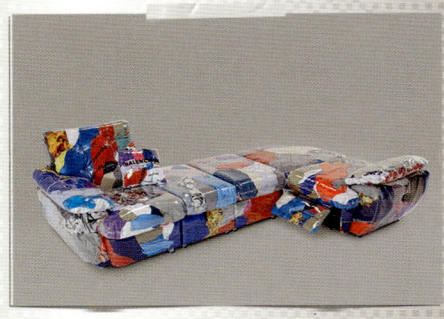

19 BALENCIAGA SOFA
186–191

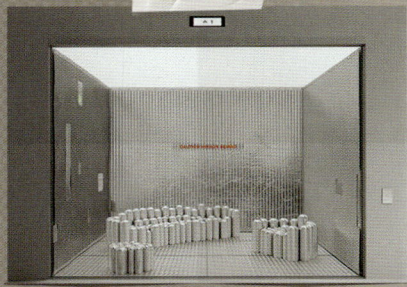

20 THE ELEVATOR AND FINGER SOFA
192–197

21 PIXEL ROOM
198–205

22 THE BEDROOM
206–211

23 CAPSULE MEETING ROOM
212–219

24 WEB-3 CAFE
220–225

25 CYBERPUNK CAFE
226–233

26 CROSBY POP-UP CAFE
234–243

27 JEWELRY STORE
244–253

28 CROSBY HOME
254–263

29 AREA STORE
264–271

30 JUST A SPACE
272–277

31 RETAIL STORE
278–283

117

Parisian Home, 2022

I have to say that after New York, Paris adds a beautiful layer to my visual language and changes the way I'm thinking. Transformation and transformism are big parts of my work, and can be seen in this project, which is my home base in Paris. As I love contrasts between different environments, I like to have them close to each other. Here, my materials, an old Parisian apartment, and street fashion come together. Inspiration for the kitchen and bedroom capsules came from corporate conference rooms. The dining and media rooms have links to my obsession with fashion. The office is inspired by my *Video Game* project around the corner from my apartment. I love my space and it really explains my feelings and language.

Purple Duplex, 2019

City life, especially in New York, definitely changes people's habits and the way they live. All of our needs can be reduced into a big changing room, a shower, and sleep depending on the day. With this project, I wanted to create an apartment that transports me to 1960s Hollywood—where it's always sunny and nobody is rushing. I used a light gray as a leading color, and added a washed purple touch. I was so in love with this carpet that I came across that I changed my mind and made these two colors equal—something I usually don't do. This duplex in Nolita was a lovely moment. After this project I began using a lot of wall-to-wall carpets.

Brooklyn Apartment, 2017

This is my fist proper apartment in Brooklyn, New York. Actually, my first apartment was only a 6.5-x-9.8-foot (2-x-3-meter) single room in Hell's Kitchen, but that's a story for another book. This project was a walk-up apartment with two bedrooms and original moldings. I had carte blanche (well not total—it was a rental) and a fresh start in Williamsburg, right before it became the Williamsburg we know today. I had two alternatives: to not take any risks and demonstrate my skills the best I could, or to go crazy and make something different. I decided to go crazy. One of my first ideas was to bring unexpected color from fashion and to customize almost every single object in an elegant but urban way. I didn't want to play with the Brooklyn-vintage-chic style, even though this apartment was asking to do so. Some of the most interesting elements are the sofa and kitchen—two things that can really shape your space and give an immediate idea of the place. I decided to do both in blue and to use unexpected finishings. Looking at this sofa, I knew I made the right decision. Taking risks and surprising yourself is very important in design.

Baby Blue Space, 2016

In high school, I had a strong fantasy about creating a monochromatic baby blue living space. My dream was to cover literally every single surface with the same color, but with different functional textures. I figured out that this apartment's installation was based on my longstanding idea only when I looked at the images from the photoshoot. This living space was one of my experiments. The 19.7-inch-wide (50-cm) staircase was my (stubborn) disagreement that I had to use the area above the bathroom for at least a library, even though you can't fully stand upstairs. This project taught me that some dreams can take a while to come true, that everything has a right time. You can work on challenging issues in many ways. The light blue color helped me make the space look bigger and a bit virtual.

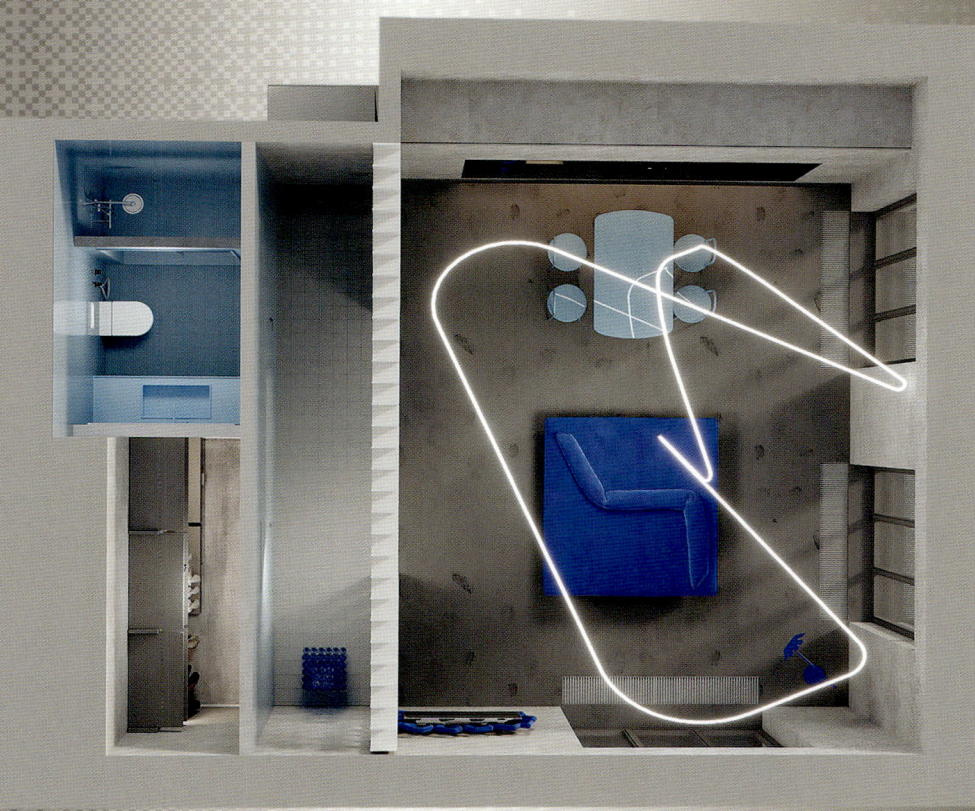

Blue Studio, 2020

Working on small living spaces is extremely important in helping us understand how much room we actually need and what our essentials are. This project consists of one small studio, a closet, and a bathroom. In the middle of the room, a convertible sofa can serve as a lounge, individual chair, or a bed. I love to use bathroom tiles for walls in living spaces. It's not what first crosses your mind when it comes to finishings, and that's why I like it.

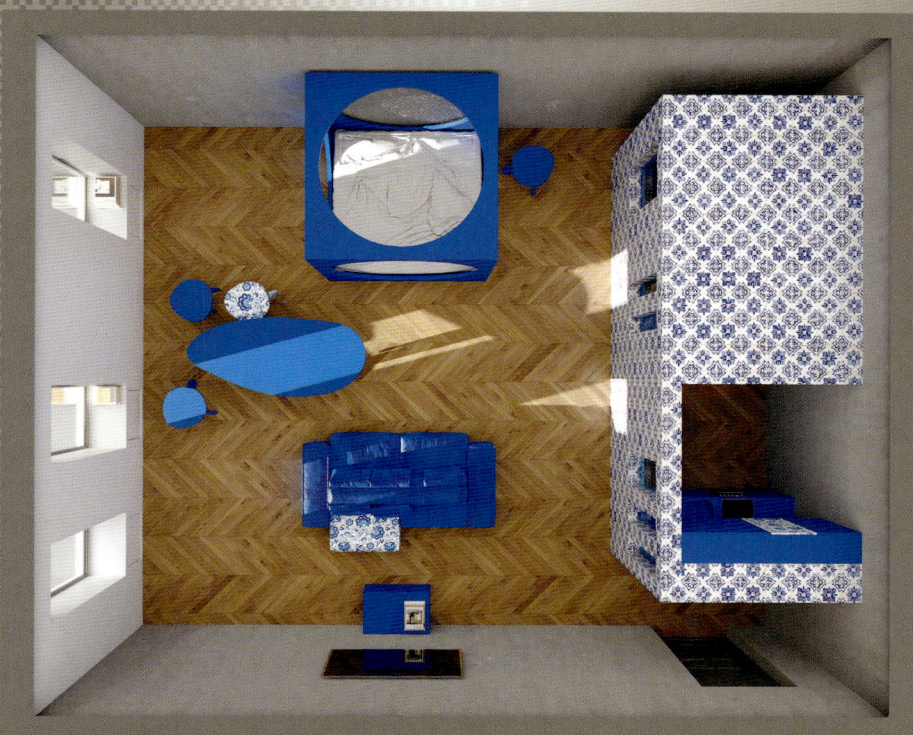

Room with Bed Capsule, 2019

Living and working in the same space is not easy. The concept behind this studio is based on daily needs. For example, during the day the space is quite formal and sharp, but at night it changes to a lounge. It elicits a relaxing mood because of the funky bed frame that looks like a futuristic mini-house or RV.

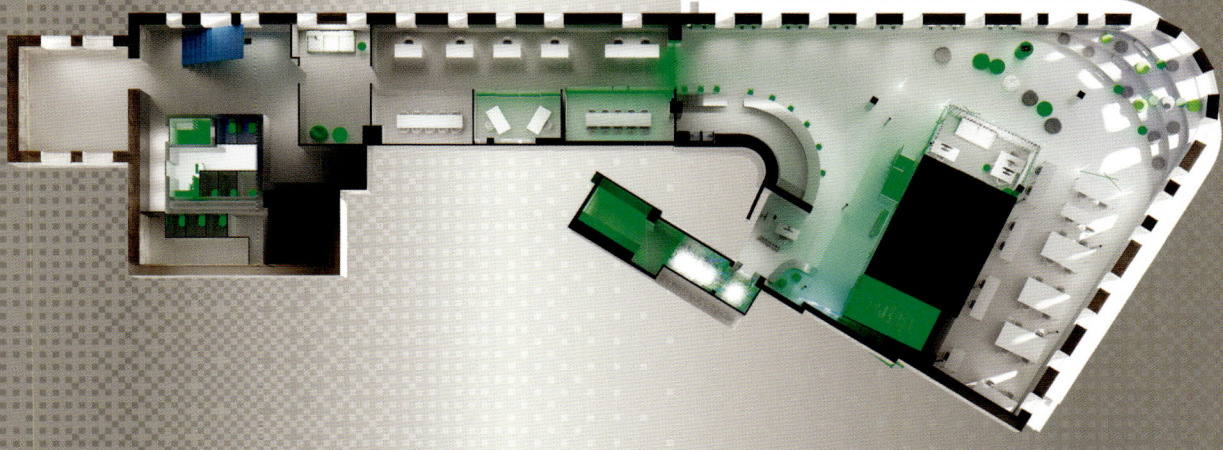

Sila Sveta Space, 2022

This project in Los Angeles was inspired by backstage spaces—what's going on behind the scenes. The combination of bright green and gray hues makes it look very futuristic. I wanted to evoke the feeling of a construction zone and backstage area. The client, Sila Sveta, a production company, regularly works on stage design, and so they were very familiar with what these kinds of spaces look like. I really like to incorporate oversized objects into my design if there is enough room for them.

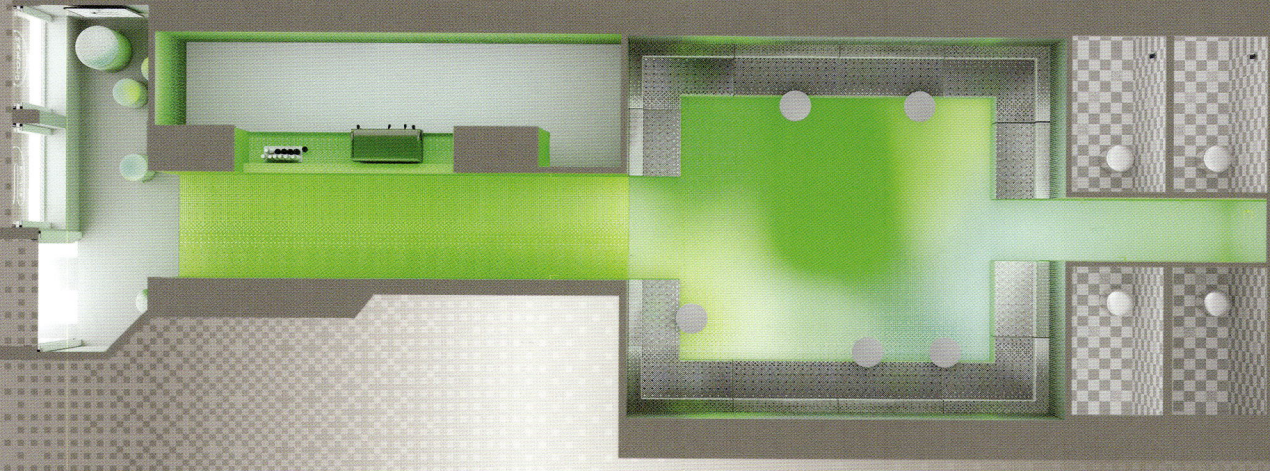

ZERO10 Pop-Up, 2022

The idea of creating a retail store that doesn't have any product in it has always been a fantasy of mine. With the help of a new technology, I figured out how to achieve this. In 2022, for New York Fashion Week, I designed this physical retail space without physical product. All the products were available in the app created by the tech company ZERO10. The interior was designed in a virtual style, meaning that everything looks like a rendering but it's actually real.

Balenciaga Sofa, 2019

One of the reasons why I decided to become an interior designer is the fashion world. I found it very strange and unfair that the interior design and furniture worlds ignore other industries except for architecture. Controversial contrast is what was missing for me. This collaboration with Balenciaga is a symbol of duality—when two ingredients that don't belong together have a dialogue and you want to be part of it. All the clothes used for the sofa were damaged or never sold, and the top cover was made out of a biodegradable film. The shape took inspiration from another time: a traditional TV recliner. All the elements, and especially the form, were reconsidered and redesigned, giving new life and second chances.

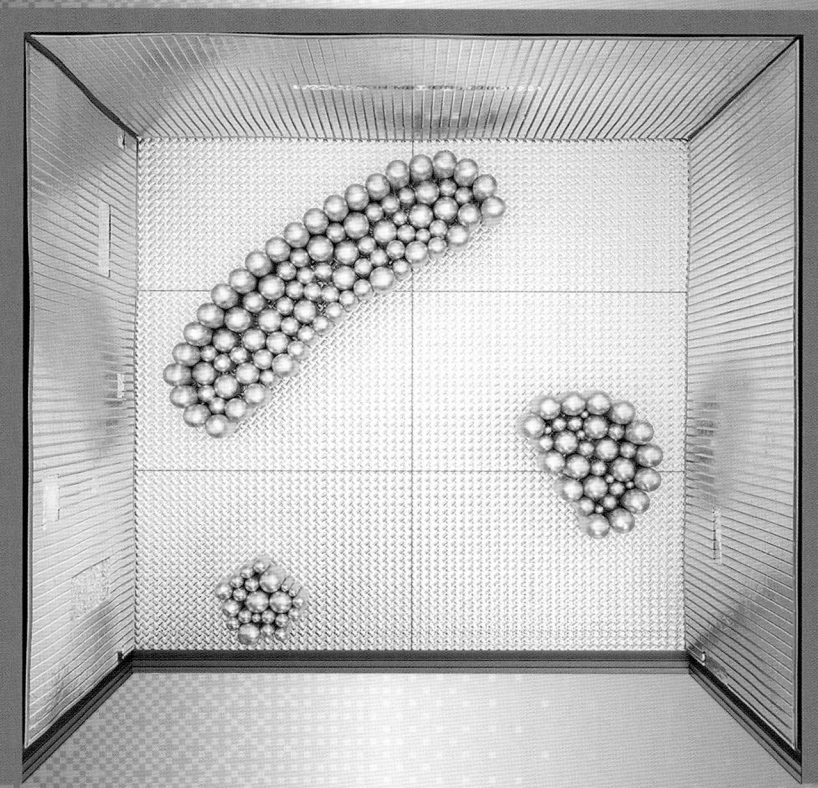

The Elevator and Finger Sofa, 2021

No one really thinks of an elevator as a room. This idea sparked *The Elevator Show* project. It's not just a room, it's also the only room that moves up and down. When you think about a room going up and down all day long, it's most likely going to be an elevator. During the show, many visitors shared their stories about elevators: awkward silences, their fears of being in a limited space, weird eye contact, and much more. When I was working on the *Finger Sofa* collection I was inspired by pieces that look like fingers. They look so good with silver.

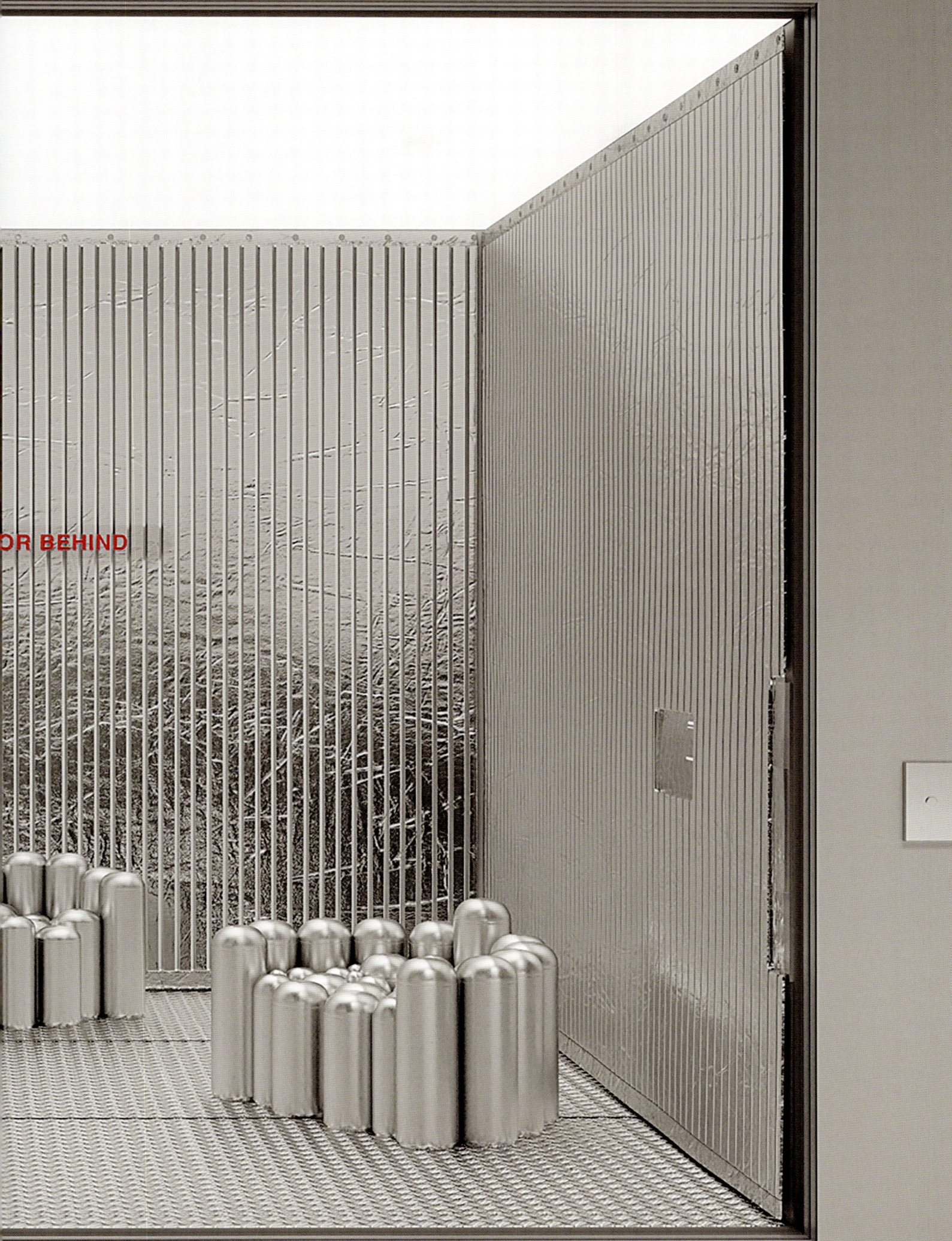

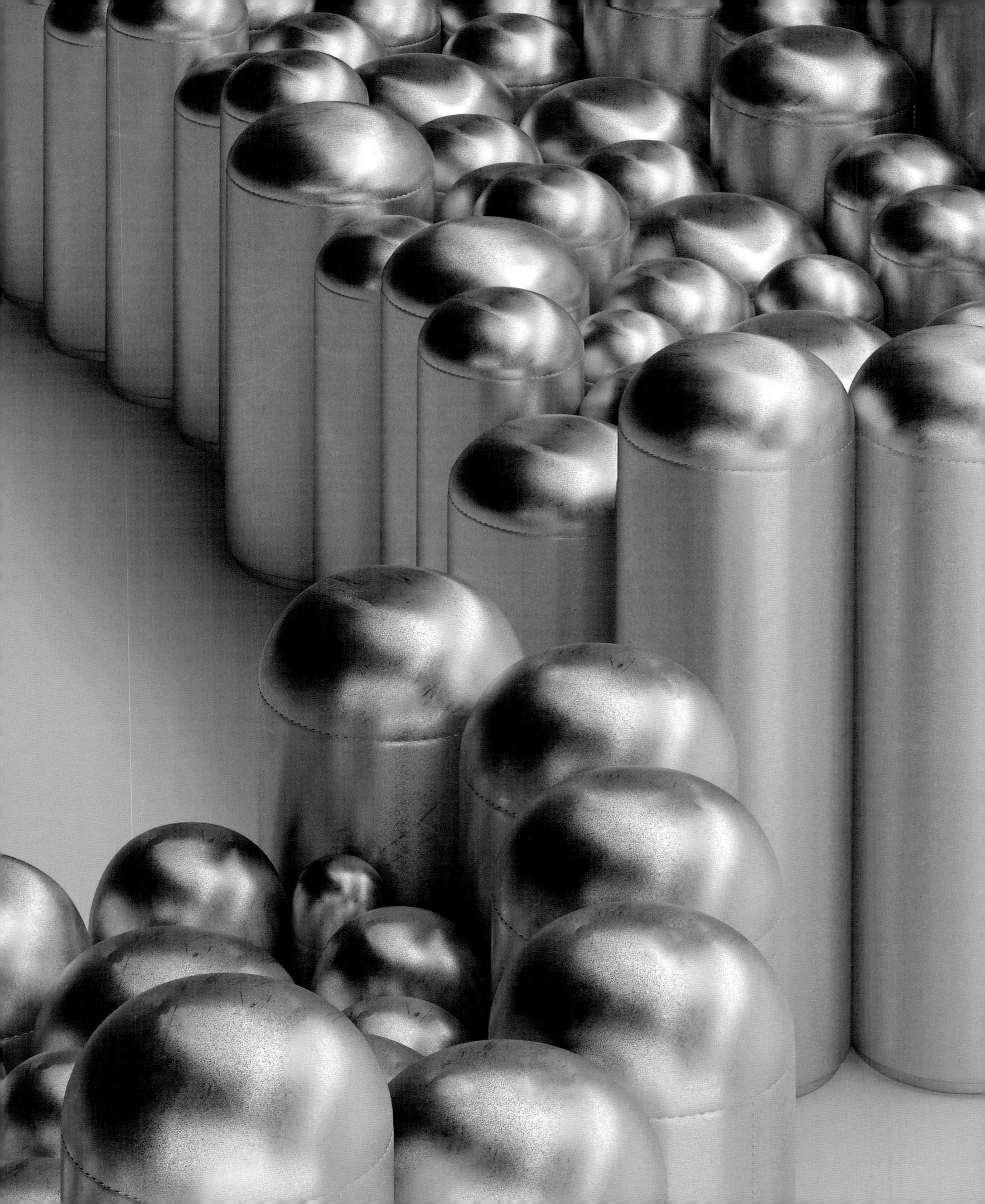

Pixel Room, 2022

This room was made during New York Design Week. I played with a pixelated style as part of my *Video Game* collection. A sofa, carpet, and little stool provide illusions of a low-resolution rendering, while objects in different shades of pink from the Moooi showroom in Midtown Manhattan are on display. This wasn't my first collaboration, but my first with a furniture brand. I love it!

The Bedroom, 2021

This project is a continuation of exploring ideas for rooms following the creation of an office, lounge, elevator, and others. This time I designed a bedroom for Design Miami. Measuring 16.4 x 16.4 feet (5 x 5 meters), the silver room features a silver mattress, a huge blanket that requires two people to move it, and an RGB-hued ceiling. From day one it ended up being a hangout room, and we had such a successful response at the fair—a mirrored bedroom in a circular shape was a real hit. I will repeat this installation in one of my residential projects in the future. Can you imagine having a proper house with flowered wallpaper and a piano, and all of a sudden finding a hidden spot like this? Art is intellectually having fun.

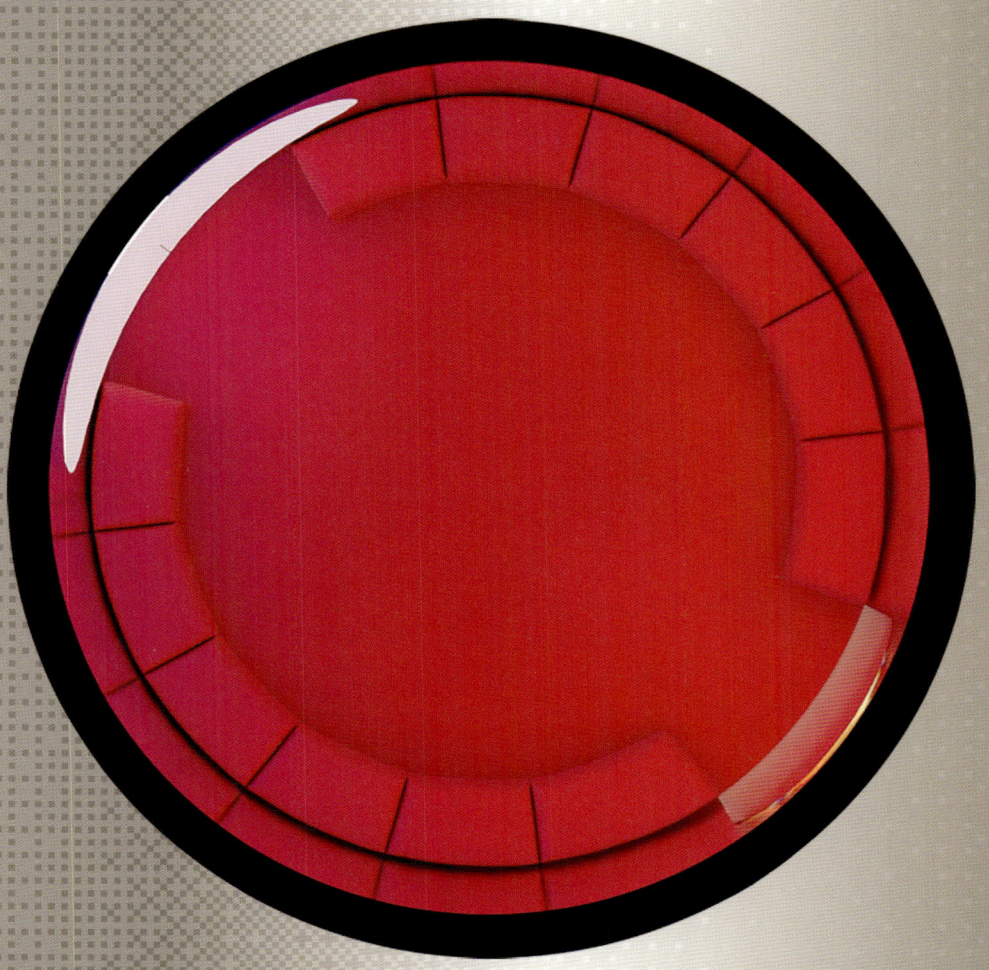

Capsule Meeting Room, 2021

The concept of working on a capsule room collection came from two different sources of inspiration. First, when I was a kid I was obsessed with kiosks, bus stations, and traffic control pavilions. For me, they were similar to tree houses and miniature worlds. Second, I was fascinated by the notion of having a freestanding room that could be placed anywhere in your house, ignoring the surroundings and style—the more different, the better. I made this particular project for an office environment, as a room for informal meetings. I can imagine this room anywhere, even in outdoor spaces.

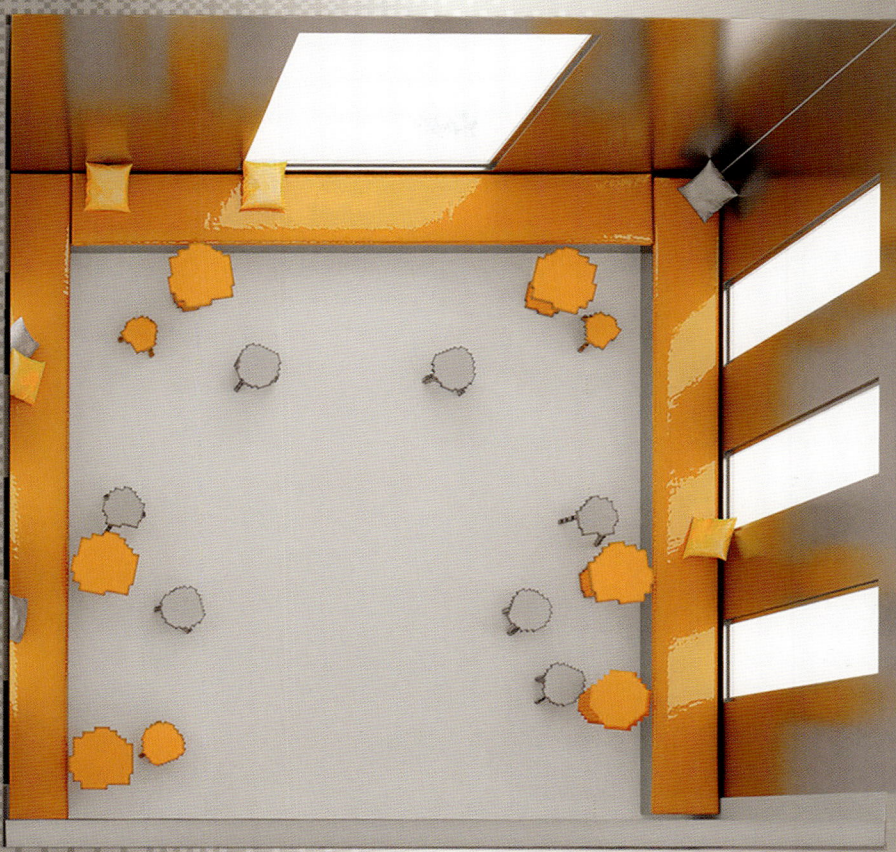

Web-3 Cafe, 2022

This project opened an absolute new style for me. I love the aesthetic of 1990s video games, which inspired me with their simplicity and playful ambiance. Working on this project, I put myself in an unusual environment because in order to create this cafe I had to use computer games instead of normal tools and technology. I created a video game first, and then designed this room from there. The immersive cafe was located in a gallery in Paris, in one of my favorite areas, Saint-Germain-des-Prés. I asked my friend Gaia Repossi to participate in the installation, which was nice because she added her unique touch with amazing music, food, and the crowd.

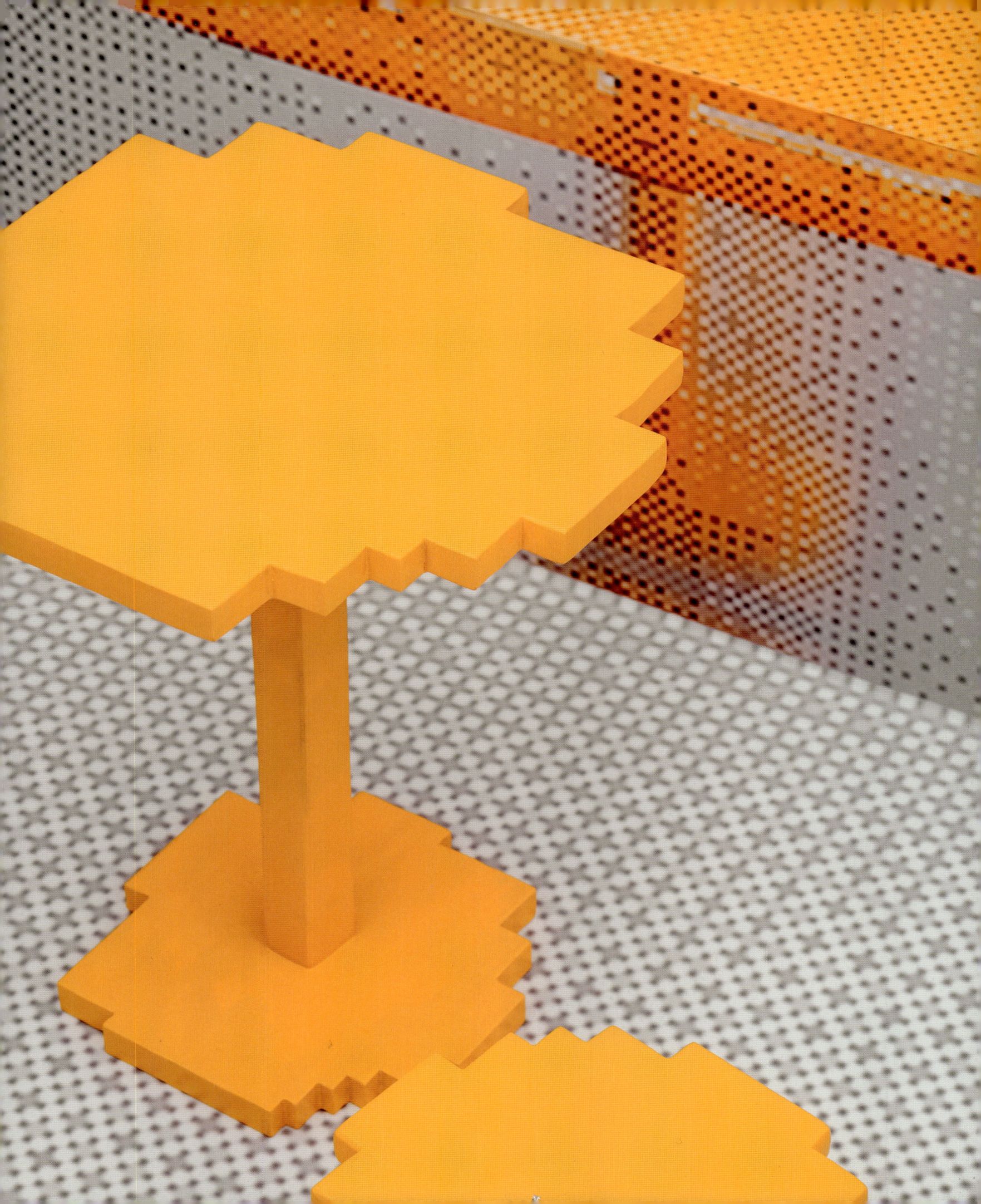

CyberPunk Cafe, 2021

This project was already in my mind back in 2015. I envisioned a cafe covered head-to-toe with stainless steel and minimalistic robots making matcha drinks. Sometimes you have to wait for the right moment to bring your idea to life. There aren't any robots, but the silver CyberPunk world landed in 2021 with one of my favorite neon-green colors.

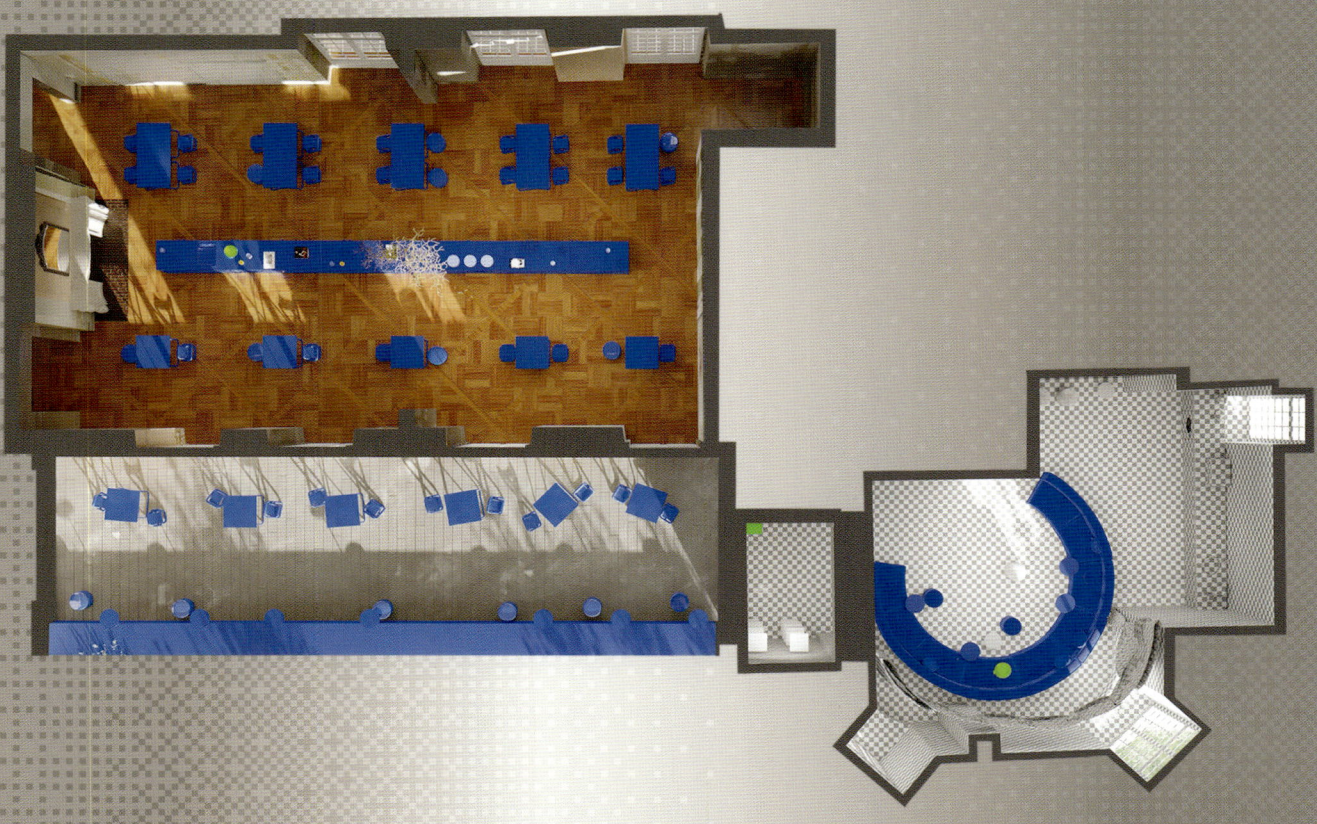

Crosby Pop-Up Cafe, 2021

Again, here is an example of the concept of transformation. I decided to use the space as it was a minute before the renovations were about to start. I really wanted to maintain the original structure and only add a couple of new details. It's a historical building with a typically Parisian style. The open kitchen here wasn't a concept; instead, it was the idea of having everyone around the place where food is prepared and cooked. I designed one room in a different way. In the digital world, gray-and-white checkers are an odd starting point. They are almost like a file with missing texture, where you can't decide what material or color should be there.

Jewelry Store, 2018–2021

For some reason, I have always felt uncomfortable in jewelry stores. Maybe I was supposed to feel uncomfortable because the employees in these boutiques didn't want people like me in there to just browse—which I was definitely doing in my early twenties. Now, times have changed and people have different shopping habits and ways of studying products. When I was working on this project, my first idea was to completely rethink the approach to jewelry retail, not necessarily only in a visual way, but mostly in the user experience. I made this store for a twenty-year-old me, who would have loved to visit the space, feel comfortable, and eventually buy a piece of jewelry.

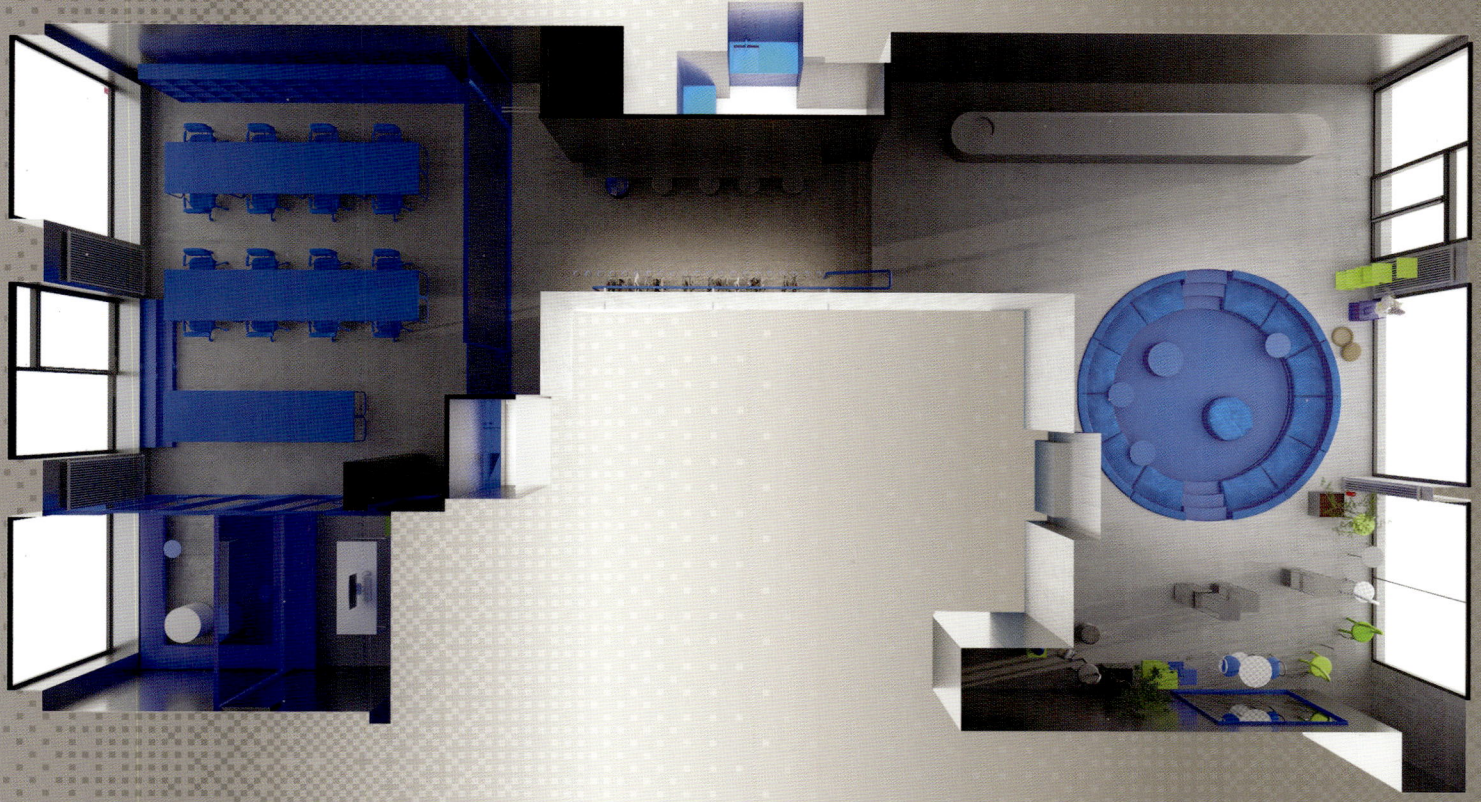

Crosby Home, 2021

When I first started Crosby Studios, I dreamed of opening a multi-national space incorporating a coffee shop, retail, my favorite magazines and books, and, most importantly, my atelier. This concept was based on the space's layout. The story starts with a large street-facing floor-to-ceiling display window, where I placed my favorite furniture I designed. Then, as you walk in, you discover a coffee and home goods shop, a spacious social area, and, eventually, the atelier. The atelier had one condition: having a huge glass door so that everyone can observe the team and daily studio routine. Seven years after launching Crosby Studios, I followed my dream to a T!

AREA Store, 2022

When you work with fashion clients who need your help representing their collections in a physical space, you are actually working as a sonography artist. Your visual skills follow the brand research. If you can understand the brand and translate it via architecture, you can't make any wrong decisions. This all-mirror store idea in New York naturally emerged after studying one of AREA's fashion collections. It sounds so obvious, but sometimes it's not that easy. You have to love or like the brand and want to wear it—otherwise it's not going to be more than just a nice store.

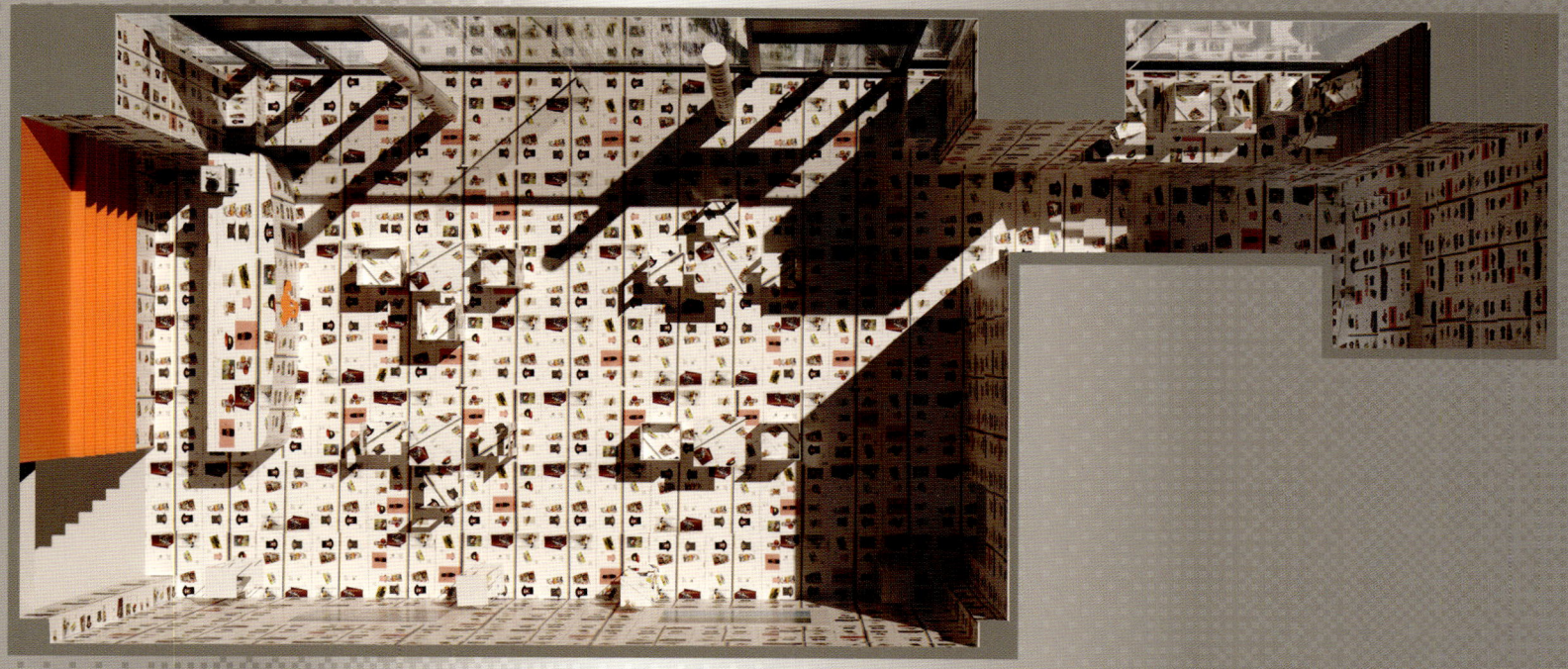

Just a Space, 2022

A couple of years before I met Sarah Andelman, I watched her documentary about Colette. It was a very inspiring two hours. When we met, I was happy to get to know Sarah and her team and to learn everything I could possibly learn. Sarah opened up another Paris I didn't know. She is truly one of the reasons why we opened a studio in Paris. For this project, Sarah asked me to design a pop-up store called *Just a Space* during Paris Fashion Week. The idea came before when we first met—I had already envisioned creating one large room and covering everything with leftover printing sheets from her book's production. Sarah helped it become reality.

Retail Store, 2022

How many stores have I visited in my life for research? I came up with my own ratings system not to compare or judge design ideas, but to feel out the space. There are many points, and I probably should write a book about them one day, but there are a couple important ones for me: feeling the newness of the environment and feeling safe at the same time. If I can perceive these two elements, the rest will come along quickly. When I design a store I don't think about walls or colors; instead, I think about how I feel in the space, and how new it is for me. For this project in Seoul, I created a 360-degree walk-through experience where customers can start and finish their browsing without missing anything.

CO-LAB

케이스티파이의 콜라보
컬렉션을 구매하는 순간부터
여러분은 크리에이티브한
케이스티파이 글로벌
커뮤니티의 멤버가 됩니다.

장르와 경계를 아우르는
다양한 브랜드와의
한정 컬렉션을
지금 바로 소장해 보세요!

CREDITS

Pages 8–9, 116, and 187–191: *The Balenciaga Sofa*, Harry Nuriev in collaboration with Balenciaga © Balenciaga; pages 8, 116, and 199–205: *Sofa So Good*, Marcel Wanders studio for Moooi © Moooi; pages 70–77: visualization, Ángel Pérez, 2021 © Ángel Pérez; pages 98–107: special thanks to Xavier Blanchot, owner of the Hôtel La Louisiane © Bienvenue Art and Hôtel La Louisiane, Paris; pages 134, 145, and 149: *Studio Object (extruded/profile)* artwork, Ian McDonald, 2014 © Studio_Ian McDonald; page 135: *Untitled / Moon Pool Project* artwork, Nikolay Koshelev, 2018 © Nikolay Koshelev; pages 135, 147, 148 and 150: *TK2001B* ceiling lamp, Tinatin Kilaberidze, 2016 © Tinatin Kilaberidze; pages 149 and 151: *Tall Oblique Vessel* artwork, Cody Hoyt, 2014 © Cody Hoyt, 2014; page 163: ceramic tiles artwork, Elena Lokastova, 2019 © Lokastova Elena; pages 166–167: Gzhel illustration, Reana M © 2010–2022 Freepik Company S.L.; Gzhel illustration, Aleksandr Tuev © 2022 Adobe, all rights reserved; pages 166–169: Gzhel illustration, pingvin_house iStock.com/pingvin_house; Gzhel illustration, Irina Zykova; pages 170–177: courtesy of Sila Sveta; pages 178–185: courtesy of Zero10, Inc.; pages 229, 231 and 233: ▍▍▐▍▍ ▐▍▍ ▍▍ digital artwork, яома _bantik, 2020 © яома _bantik; pages 244–253: courtesy of Avgvst; pages 274–275: *Futures Tennis Close* (2018) and *Thalia Beach, Friday No. 2* (2019) photographs from the series *Uncrowded Fields*, and *Northeastern Volleyball* (2018) and *Dartmouth Basketall* (2019) photographs from the series *Crowded Fields*, Pelle Cass; pages 274–275 and 277: Café Nuances; pages 278–283: courtesy of Casetify.

PHOTOGRAPHS

11h45: pages 236–239, 241.
Julie Ansiau: pages 274–277.
Jeanne Michelle Canto: pages 208–211.
Dylan Chandler: pages 134–141 and 266–271; pages 214–219, courtesy of Instagram.
Benoît Florençon: pages 120–131, 222–225, 240, and 242–243.
James Harris: pages 194–197.
Vasiliy Hurtin: pages 172–177.
Inna Kablukova: pages 5 (bottom), 16 (top), and 188–191.
Mikhail Loskutov: pages 144–151, 154–157, 160–163, 166–169, 228–233, 246–249, 252–253, and 256–263.
Robin Noordam, courtesy of Moooi: pages 200–205.
Eric Petschek: pages 180–185.
Daniel Roché: page 6.
Dmitrii Tsyrenshchikov: pages 250 and 251.

ACKNOWLEDGMENTS

Once, a long time ago, I asked a very successful friend what was the secret behind her incredibly fortunate fate. Her response changed my life: "Fate has names." I'd like to thank the individuals behind the fate of this book.

Thank you Catherine Bonifassi for believing in my work and guiding me throughout this journey, and to Charles Miers for making it happen.

Thank you Sarah Andelman, for your continued inspiration, authentic kindness, and friendship.

Thank you Samir Bantal for motivating me to be a better artist, for your vision of life, and for your friendship and support.

Thank you Aurélie Julien for your encouragement, insights, critical eye, and motivation while accompanying me throughout every project, and for our friendship and family.

Thank you Julien Lombrail, Loïc Le Gaillard, and Léa Meunier for your amazing sense of community, support, and amity.

Thank you to all the members of the amazing Cassi Edition and Rizzoli New York teams—Vanessa Blondel, Candice Guillaume, Lou-Ann Thual, and Victorine Lamothe—for your expertise, professionalism, and patience.

And thank you to my lovely Crosby Studios team—Maria Begun, Anastasiia Pestrikova, Zhanna Ee, Polina Velikova, Nina Neserina, Aleksandr Konkov, Alina Ivakhno, Maria Udalova, Olga Voronchihina, William Luck, and Maria Smirnova—for your talent and incredible hard work; I couldn't have made it happen without you.

And of course thank you to all my clients and partners who believed in me and provided me with the chance to build it all. This book would have never happened without you. And thank you to all the editors who have helped make my work visible and for giving it a voice—this is very important for us.

Finally, a very special thank you to my family and my partner, Tyler Billinger, for being by my side.

—Harry Nuriev

How to Land in the Metaverse:
From Interior Design to the Future of Design

First published in the United States of America in 2023 by
Rizzoli International Publications, Inc.
300 Park Avenue South
New York, NY 10010
www.rizzoliusa.com

© CROSBY STUDIOS LLC

Foreword: Sarah Andelman
Introduction: Samir Bantal
Texts: Harry Nuriev

Publisher: Charles Miers
Editorial Director: Catherine Bonifassi
Editor: Victorine Lamothe
Production Director: Maria Pia Gramaglia
Managing Editor: Lynn Scrabis

Artistic Direction: Crosby Studios

Editorial Coordination:
Cassi Edition
Vanessa Blondel, Candice Guillaume

All rights reserved. No part of this publication may be reproduced, stored in a retrieval system, or transmitted in any form or by any means, electronic, mechanical, photocopying, recording, or otherwise, without prior consent of the publisher.

ISBN: 978-0-8478-7258-9
Library of Congress Control Number: 2022946163
2023 2024 2025 2026 / 10 9 8 7 6 5 4 3 2 1
Printed in Hong Kong

Visit us online:
Facebook.com/RizzoliNewYork
Twitter: @Rizzoli_Books
Instagram.com/RizzoliBooks
Pinterest.com/RizzoliBooks
Youtube.com/user/RizzoliNY
Issuu.com/Rizzoli